To get started with this book, you'll need:

- micro:bit (BBC Micro:bit)
- computer or laptop with a proper keyboard
- internet connection
- microUSB cable

Other items you'll need to enjoy all the projects are listed on page 4. You don't have to buy them all now — items you'll need for each project are indicated at the start of each one, so you can obtain these as you progress through the book.

It is recommended that children should be supervised when using the internet, especially when using a new website. The publishers and the author cannot be held responsible for the content of the websites referred to in this book.

Anyone who is interested in coding will love this book!

 micro:bit

© Copyright Micro:bit Educational Foundation or Foundation partners.

The QuestKids® series is an imprint of In Easy Steps Limited
16 Hamilton Terrace, Holly Walk, Leamington Spa, Warwickshire, United Kingdom CV32 4LY
www.ineasysteps.com
www.thequestkids.com

ISBN: 978-1-78791-000-3

MIX
Paper from responsible sources
FSC
www.fsc.org   FSC® C020837

Printed and bound in the United Kingdom

Notice of Liability
Every effort has been made to ensure that this book contains accurate and current information. However, In Easy Steps Limited and the authors shall not be liable for any loss or damage suffered by readers as a result of any information contained herein.

Contributors:
Author: Dan Aldred
Creative Designer: Jo Cowan
Editor: Belinda Gallagher
Cover & character illustrations: Marcelo (The Bright Agency)

Acknowledgements
The publisher would like to thank the following sources for the use of their illustrations:
Backgrounds: iStock
Teachwithict.com: 57 (temperature sensor)
Illustrations courtesy of the following Pixabay artists: 16 (computer) 200 Degrees;
29 (pause button) OpenClipart-Vectors;
42 & 43 (landscapes) M. Maggs;
52 (hand) Htc Erl; 56 (arrows);
61 (thermometers) Clker-Free-Vector-Images;
62 (LEDs) Sinisa Maric;
65 (loudspeaker) sumansarkar;
73 (crystal ball) Gerren Rabideau;
77 (compass) OpenClipart-Vectors;
84 (radio waves) Clker-Free-Vector-Images;
90 (backpack) OpenClipart-Vectors

Every effort has been made to acknowledge the source and copyright holder of each picture. In Easy Steps Limited apologises for any unintentional errors or omissions.

Contents

Let's see what we can do together!

Welcome to micro:bit coding

To get the best out of this book we encourage you to read it in page order to gain the maximum knowledge and skills. Pages 6-15 will help you get familiar with the micro:bit and the online coding editor you will use to create code. Then you'll move on to learning three skill sets. These skills are needed for you to progress to the projects. Most of all, have fun as you go!

WHAT YOU'LL NEED FOR THE PROJECTS

- For some projects two micro:bits are required
- 2 x battery packs
- 4 x AAA batteries
- 4 x crocodile clips with wires
- An LED
- An elastic or rubber band
- Temperature sensor TMP36
- Foil
- A speaker or headphones
- Your school bag

SKILLS AND PROJECTS

There are 10 interactive projects for you to try. At the start of each one is a panel with the skills you'll learn and the equipment needed. Then there is a simple, visual set of instructions to follow, with some theory to explain how things work. All the code is given to you, so even if you've never programmed before, you'll be able to follow along. Here's a quick breakdown of your book:

SKILL SETS

1 > **Getting started** This gives you a tour of the micro:bit and gets you started with coding your first program.
2 > **Basics** Here, you'll learn how to display images and text on the micro:bit's LED grid.
3 > **Inputs** Get to grips with the input systems such as the buttons, accelerometer, and light sensor.

PROJECTS

1 > The 99 game This project is a game of chance that involves throwing the micro:bit among a group of friends. You'll learn more about coding, like using variables and control flow techniques.

2 > Heads or tails You'll use the LED grid and accelerometer to create a "coin-toss" generator that detects when you flip the micro:bit, and it displays heads or tails.

3 > Steady hand game This game challenges you to hold the micro:bit in your hand as long as you can without wobbling. You'll learn more about the micro:bit's abilities and other fundamental coding techniques.

4 > Temperature display Use the built-in temperature sensor to detect the temperature and scroll it across the LED grid.

5 > LED control Learn how to wire up an external LED and control it with code. This exercise teaches you about using the micro:bit with other components so you can build even bigger projects.

6 > Trespasser alarm By connecting a speaker to the micro:bit, you'll create an alarm system that detects when someone has broken into your room, and alerts you by playing a tune.

7 > Fortune teller This project ramps up the coding complexity, showing you how to program your micro:bit to tell your fortune just like a Magic 8 ball!

8 > Compass Turn the micro:bit into a real working compass using its built-in magnetometer.

9 > Radio communication Use two micro:bits to send and receive radio messages.

10 > Bag alarm Using your radio skills from the previous project, combined with the accelerometer, you'll build a bag alarm with two micro:bits. The first micro:bit stays inside your bag and alerts a second micro:bit in your pocket if someone tries to steal your bag.

Let's get reading!

PLUGGING IN YOUR MICRO:BIT

1 Plug the microUSB cable into the port located at the top of your micro:bit.

2 Plug the other end of the cable into a USB port on your computer or laptop. The micro:bit will power up.

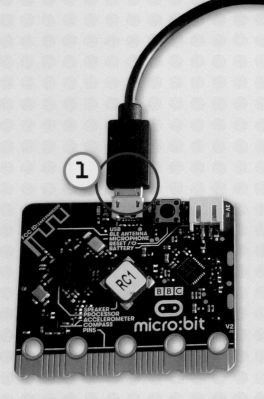

The first time you plug in a new micro:bit, it will run a simple program to introduce you to some of its features, such as pressing buttons, shaking the micro:bit, and chasing dots of light.

The micro:bit can hold only one program at a time, so when you write your own programs you'll overwrite this introductory program.

If you want to reinstall it, download the file from **https://bit.ly/31GpoAp**

USING THE MAKECODE EDITOR

Open your web browser (Chrome or Edge is recommended), enter the address **https://makecode.microbit.org**, and click **New Project**. This will take you to the **MakeCode editor** where you can drag and drop **coding blocks** onto the coding area. These blocks snap together to create a program that can be converted into JavaScript or Python code.

The advantage of using blocks is that you don't have to worry about typos or syntax; the blocks take care of that. You'll create your program code using this editor, which will automatically save your progress in your web browser so you can access it again later. You'll then download your programs so you can transfer them to the micro:bit.

Let's look at a few aspects of the MakeCode editor on page 7.

Running the simulator

The MakeCode editor has a **micro:bit simulator**, so even if you don't yet have an actual micro:bit you can still write programs and run them. The simulator runs your programs as if it were a real micro:bit — you can even shake it, press its buttons, and attach virtual headphones to it.

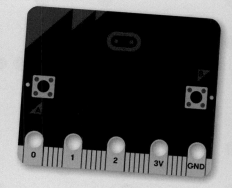

Navigating the coding interface

Here's a quick overview of the MakeCode editor and what each button does:

The simulator is a great tool for testing your programs work before you download them to the micro:bit.

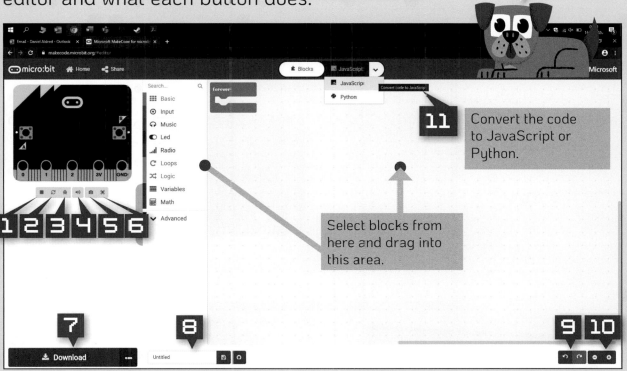

11 Convert the code to JavaScript or Python.

Select blocks from here and drag into this area.

1 Stop the micro:bit simulator

2 Reset the simulator

3 Enter debugging mode to run the program in slow motion and fix any errors before downloading it

4 Mute the audio playing through your computer's speakers

5 Run the simulator in full-screen mode

6 Take a screenshot of the micro:bit display

7 Download the program file

8 Rename and save the program file

9 Undo or redo the last block

10 Zoom in or out of the programming window

11 Convert your code to JavaScript or Python

Running your code on the micro:bit

Once you've written and tested a program, you'll want to run it on a real micro:bit. When you click the **Download** button, the MakeCode editor will connect to your micro:bit and attempt to write the program code to your micro:bit.

By default, the file will be given a random name, usually *microbit-Untitled.hex* but it's a good idea to give your project a descriptive name to make it easier to locate the file later. To rename the file, enter a new project name in the **Untitled** text box and then click **Download**.

When you click **Download**, you will be asked to connect and pair a micro:bit. This only needs to be done the first time that you connect.

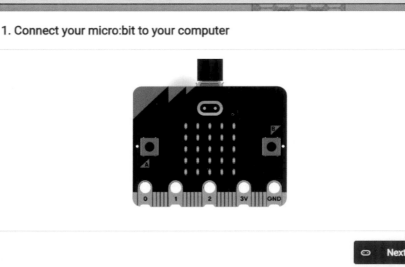

1. Connect your micro:bit to your computer

Next

If you haven't already, plug your micro:bit into one of the USB ports on your device. Then click the **Next** button.

micro:bit plugged into a USB port

You will be asked to pair the micro:bit. This simply means to join the micro:bit to your computer so you can transfer code. Press the **Pair** button.

The following window will load. Select BBC micro:bit from the list and then press the **Connect** button.

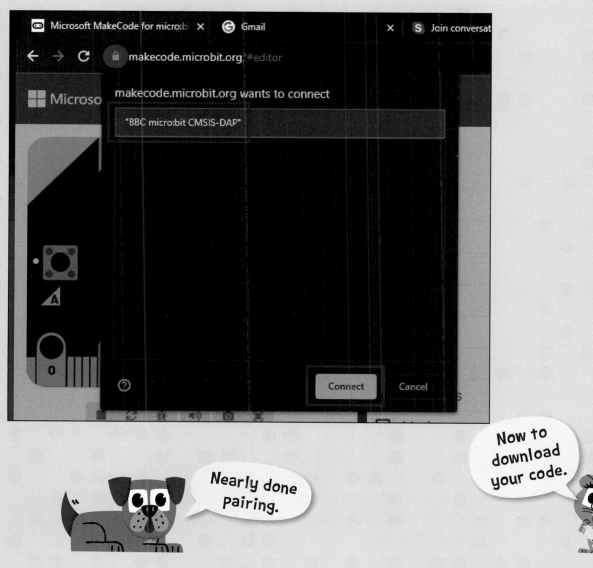

Nearly done Pairing.

Now to download your code.

Once successfully paired you will see the window below. Press the **Download** button to write the program to your micro:bit.

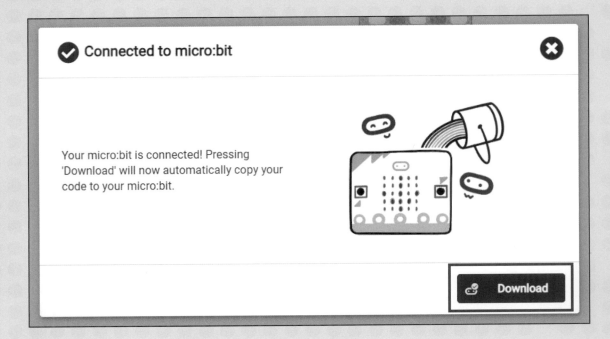

The **Let's code** window will display this downloading page.

Your program will download. Check out your micro:bit.

On the back of the micro:bit is a single red LED. When it is on, it means the micro:bit is powered. A flashing LED indicates your program is being written to the micro:bit.

Red LED

Once the program is downloaded, the LED will stop flashing. Turn the micro:bit over to use your program.

To restart the program, simply press the **Reset** button on the back.

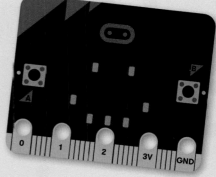

Reset button

USB
BLE ANTENNA
MICROPHONE

Next time you write your program code to the micro:bit, simply press the **Download** button — there's no need to pair.

Click Download.

Sometimes you might want to download the program to your computer first. Without the micro:bit plugged in, press **Download**. You will see the screen below and the file will be saved to your *Downloads* folder.

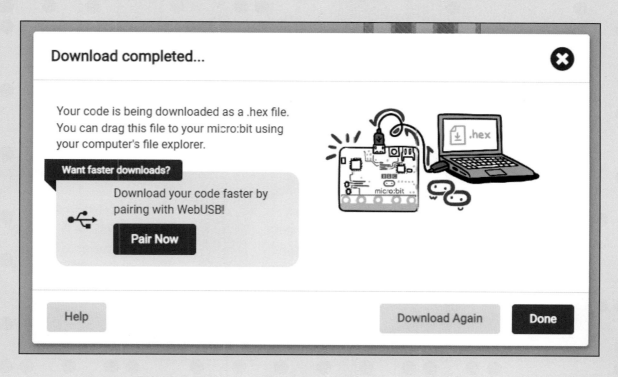

Download completed...

Your code is being downloaded as a .hex file. You can drag this file to your micro:bit using your computer's file explorer.

Want faster downloads?

Download your code faster by pairing with WebUSB!

Pair Now

Help   Download Again   Done

Open your *Downloads* folder and locate your program file. It should have the name you gave it, and the *.hex* extension.

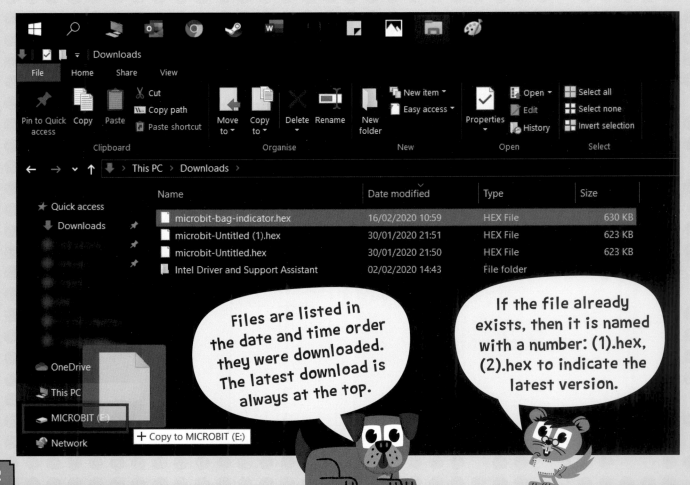

When you plugged in the micro:bit, your computer should have registered it as a drive. That means you should see MICROBIT in the Quick access panel on the left of your screen. Drag the *.hex* file over to the MICROBIT drive (see below) to start downloading the program to the micro:bit. You will see a flashing LED on the back of the micro:bit. This indicates the file is transferring successfully.

Files are listed in the date and time order they were downloaded. The latest download is always at the top.

If the file already exists, then it is named with a number: (1).hex, (2).hex to indicate the latest version.

Uploading code

When you return to the MakeCode editor site, it should automatically display a list of projects that you've previously written and saved, as shown below.

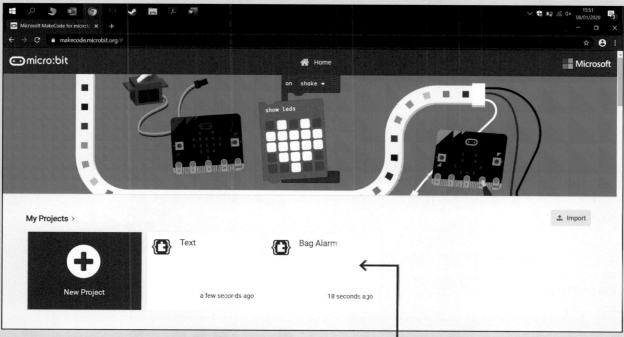

Click the name of the program that you want to open.

You can also drag and drop the .hex files from your *Downloads* folder into the coding area to load an old project, as shown below.

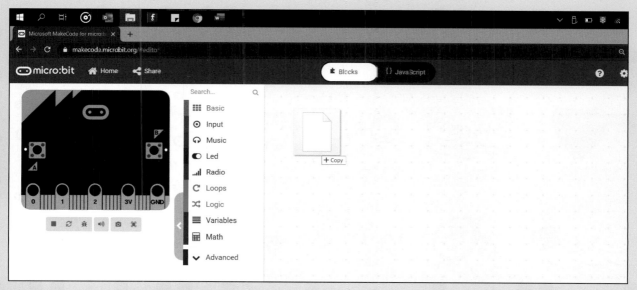

Loading a saved project

NOTE: It is not always possible to load the program file from the micro:bit hardware, so ensure that you save a separate copy on your computer.

OTHER SETTINGS

Project Settings

Extensions

Print...

Delete Project

Language

High Contrast On

Green Screen On

Report Abuse...

Reset

About...

The MakeCode editor gives you some options to customize it to your liking. Click the gear icon at the top right of the page to access these settings.

Here, you can print your project, delete it, and add code blocks that other people have written (that is, blocks that aren't built into the editor).

You can also set the language of the blocks to match yours.

Accessing the MakeCode editor's settings

OTHER PROJECT IDEAS

On the MakeCode website you'll find a number of fun projects that other users have made (see below). To try one out, simply click the project and the required program blocks will load. You can then download or edit the program.

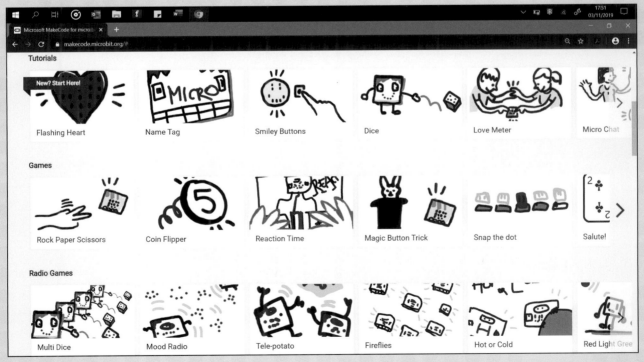

Projects made by other users

OTHER WAYS TO PROGRAM THE MICRO:BIT

The MakeCode editor is not the only way to program the micro:bit; there are several different editors that let you code in another programming language. Head over to **https://microbit.org/code/** and you'll find a text-based version of Python to write programs for your micro:bit:

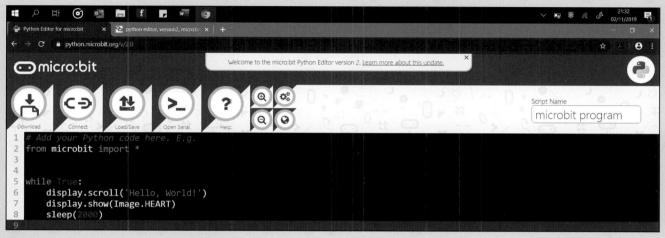

A different kind of micro:bit code editor

There are also other third-party programming editors that you can use to choose other languages and coding methods, shown below. For a complete list, visit **https://microbit.org/code-alternative-editors/**

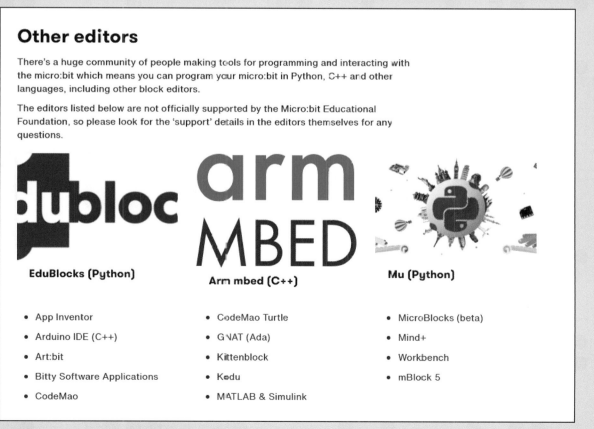

Other editors

There's a huge community of people making tools for programming and interacting with the micro:bit which means you can program your micro:bit in Python, C++ and other languages, including other block editors.

The editors listed below are not officially supported by the Micro:bit Educational Foundation, so please look for the 'support' details in the editors themselves for any questions.

EduBlocks (Python)

Arm mbed (C++)

Mu (Python)

- App Inventor
- Arduino IDE (C++)
- Art:bit
- Bitty Software Applications
- CodeMao

- CodeMao Turtle
- GNAT (Ada)
- Kittenblock
- Kodu
- MATLAB & Simulink

- MicroBlocks (beta)
- Mind+
- Workbench
- mBlock 5

Other options for coding the micro:bit

SKILL SET 1
Getting started

It's time to get familiar with the micro:bit features and hardware. You'll also learn how to access the MakeCode editor to write your first program.

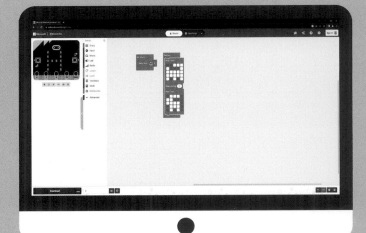

IN THIS SKILL SET

1. **Meet the micro:bit**
2. **Get connected**
3. **Access the coding interface**
4. **Explore the MakeCode editor**
5. **Start a program**
6. **Show a string**
7. **Use the micro:bit simulator**
8. **Write the program to your micro:bit**
9. **View the JavaScript or Python code**

Are you ready to take a closer look at the micro:bit?

1 Meet the micro:bit

Get to know the micro:bit.

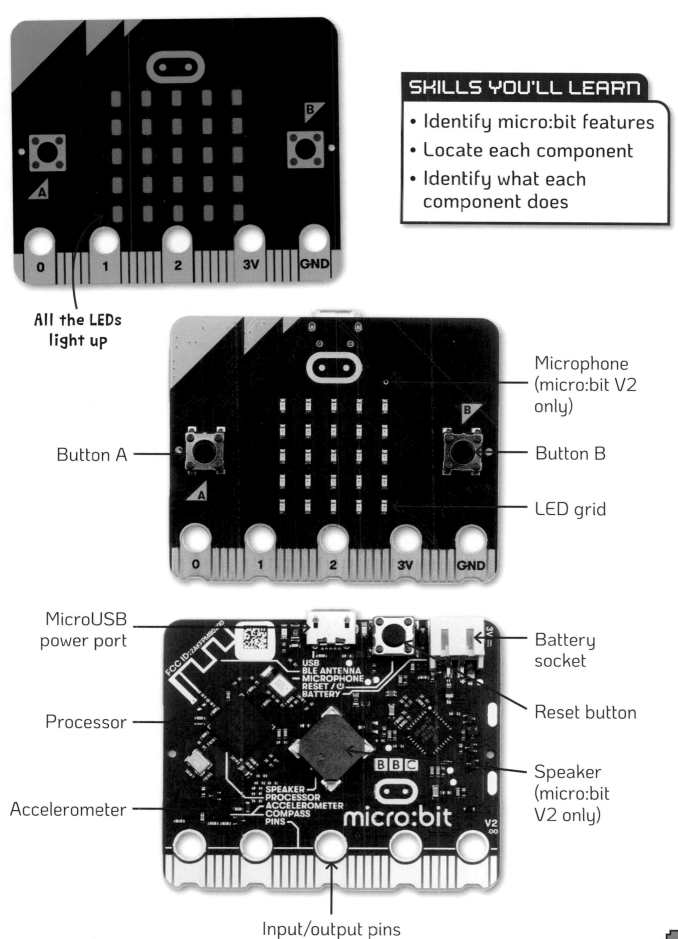

SKILLS YOU'LL LEARN

- Identify micro:bit features
- Locate each component
- Identify what each component does

All the LEDs light up

Microphone (micro:bit V2 only)

Button A

Button B

LED grid

MicroUSB power port

Battery socket

Processor

Reset button

Accelerometer

Speaker (micro:bit V2 only)

Input/output pins

2 Get connected

Power the micro:bit with the computer or the battery pack.

SKILLS YOU'LL LEARN

- Attach a battery pack
- Attach the microUSB cable

Get powered up!

HOW TO DO IT

Connect the microUSB cable and computer

Attach the smaller end of the microUSB cable to the microUSB slot on the micro:bit. Connect the other end of the cable to a computer. You should hear a beep and see the *MICROBIT* folder open on your screen.

Connect the battery pack

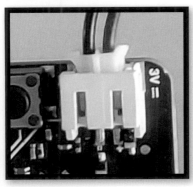

Some projects require the micro:bit to be portable so you can use it away from your computer. For these, you'll need to use the battery pack and two AAA batteries.

First, write your program and download it to the micro:bit, then unplug the micro:bit from the computer. Add both batteries to the battery pack and connect it, via the wire connector, to the micro:bit's battery socket.

Once attached, the batteries power the micro:bit. Save battery life by removing the pack when you've finished using the micro:bit. Hold the white socket and gently move it from side to side to release it. Do not pull the wire, it might break. **You cannot code the micro:bit while it's running on battery power; it must be connected to a computer.**

3 Access the coding interface

Visit the micro:bit website to get started with coding.

SKILLS YOU'LL LEARN

- Access the micro:bit MakeCode editor

Connect the micro:bit to your computer. Go to **https://microbit.org/**

HOW TO DO IT

Click **Let's code** at the top of the page, then click **Go to MakeCode editor**.

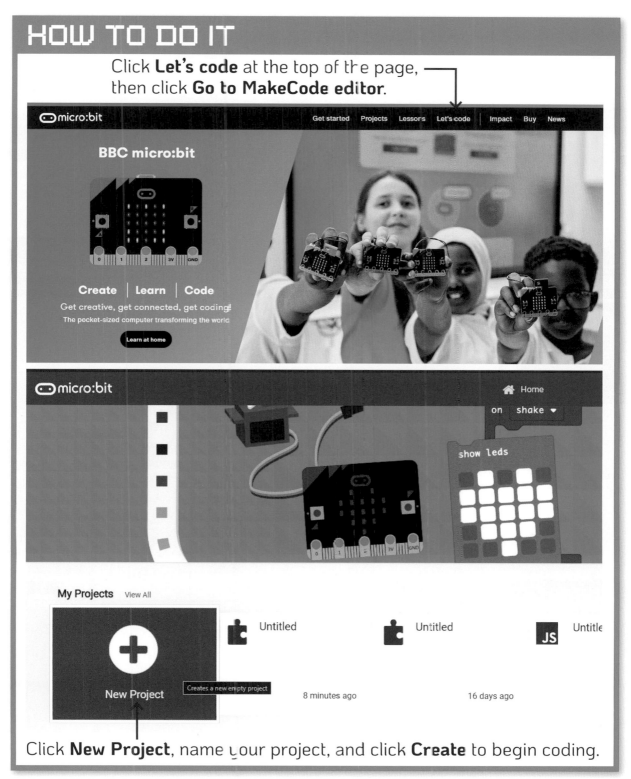

Click **New Project**, name your project, and click **Create** to begin coding.

4 Explore the MakeCode editor

Become familiar with the MakeCode editor coding interface.

SKILLS YOU'LL LEARN

• Navigate the coding interface

The MakeCode editor is clear and easy to use. Explore its features below.

HOW TO DO IT

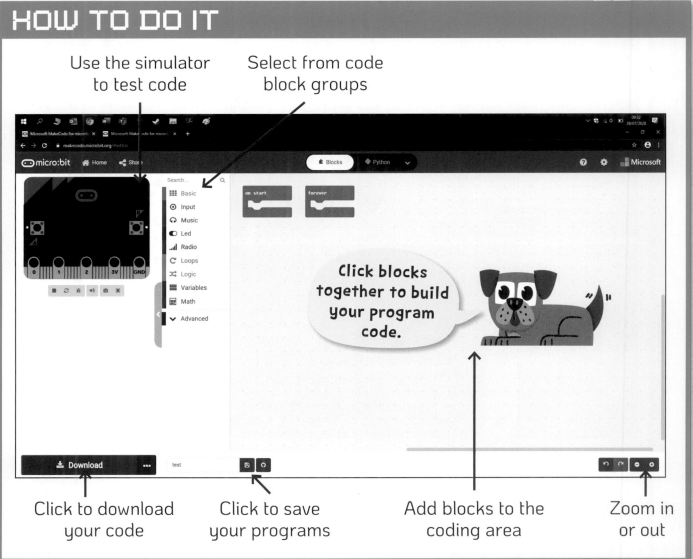

Use the simulator to test code

Select from code block groups

Click blocks together to build your program code.

Click to download your code

Click to save your programs

Add blocks to the coding area

Zoom in or out

5 Start a program

Begin writing your first program for the micro:bit.

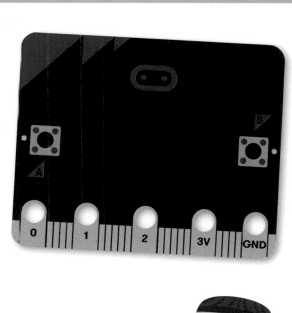

SKILLS YOU'LL LEARN

- Write a micro:bit program

GET YOUR BLOCKS

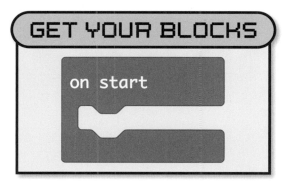

on start

Blocks snap together to help you create code.

PUT IT TOGETHER

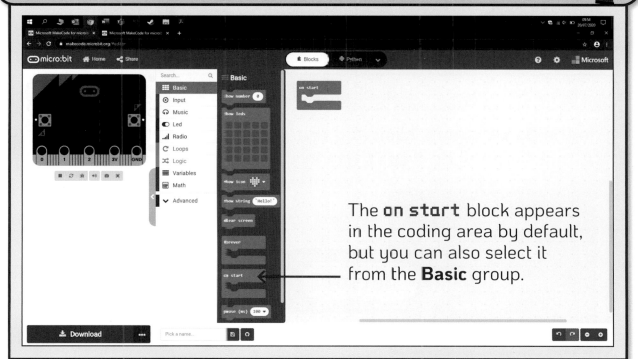

The **on start** block appears in the coding area by default, but you can also select it from the **Basic** group.

THEORY

The **on start** block tells the micro:bit to perform the action in the code when the program starts.

6 Show a string

Complete the micro:bit program from the previous step to scroll a custom message across the LED grid.

SKILLS YOU'LL LEARN

• Create a string

WHAT YOU'LL NEED

• Battery pack

GET YOUR BLOCKS

show string " Hello! "

Each letter of the string is scrolled across the display.

PUT IT TOGETHER

In the **Basic** group, click and drag the **show string** block. Attach it to the **on start** block.

on start

show string " Hello! "

Change the string from **Hello!** to your own message.

THEORY

The **show string** block scrolls a *string* — a series of text, digits, and symbols — of your choosing across the LED grid.

7 Use the micro:bit simulator

Watch your message scroll by on the MakeCode editor's micro:bit simulator.

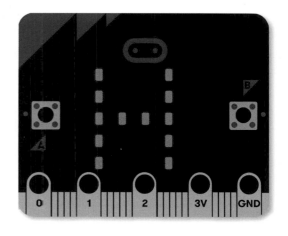

SKILLS YOU'LL LEARN

- Run code on the simulator
- Change the speed of the simulator

HOW TO DO IT

Click the button, and you'll see your message scrolling across the micro:bit simulator.

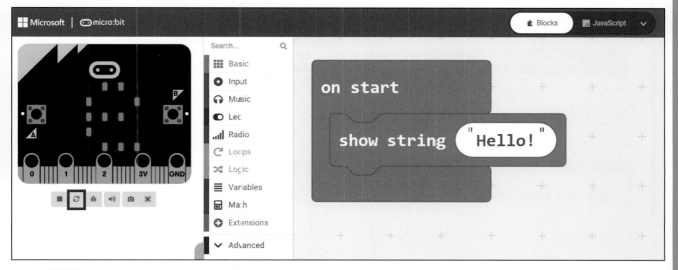

The button helps you *debug* (check for errors in) the code. It lets you turn on slow motion and see more clearly what your program code is doing.

Use the button to make the simulation fullscreen.

8 Write the program to your micro:bit

Transfer the scrolling message program to your micro:bit.

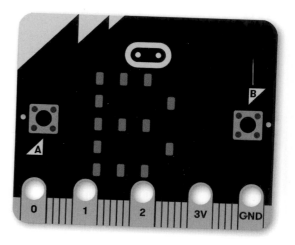

HOW TO DO IT

Click the **Download** button at the bottom left of the screen. The button will turn green, and the MakeCode editor will download the program code onto your micro:bit.

The orange light on the back of your micro:bit will flash as the program is written to it.

OPTIONAL: Remove the micro:bit from the computer and add the battery pack (see page 18).

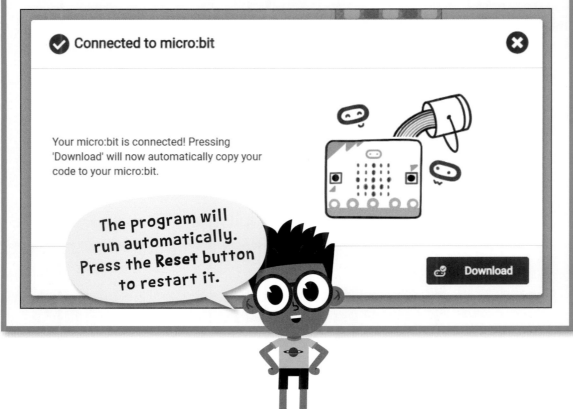

The program will run automatically. Press the **Reset** button to restart it.

9 View the JavaScript or Python code

See how the code blocks translate into the JavaScript or Python programming languages.

HOW TO DO IT

The coding blocks can be converted into two popular programming languages called *JavaScript* and *Python*, which are often used in websites, games and mobile phone apps.

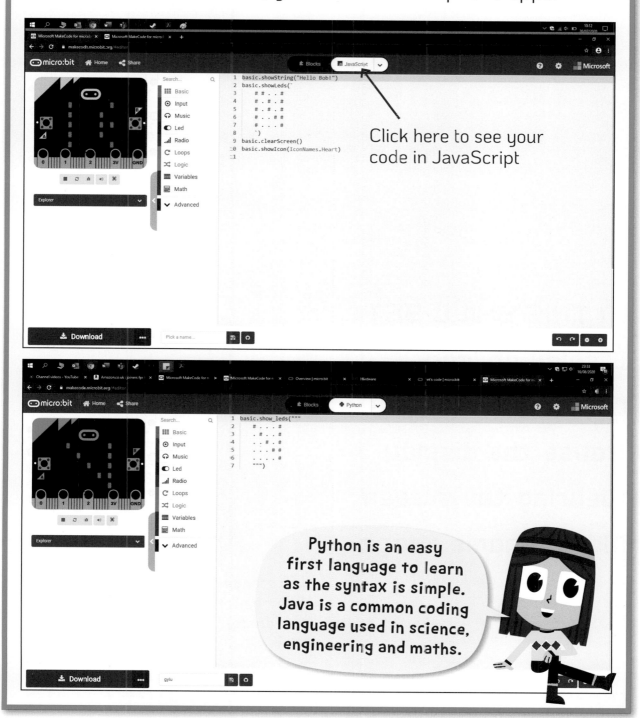

Click here to see your code in JavaScript

Python is an easy first language to learn as the syntax is simple. Java is a common coding language used in science, engineering and maths.

SKILL SET 2
Basics

This skill set covers how to use the LED grid to display images and how to program your own images using blocks from the Basic group. You'll combine these skills to create a personalized name badge.

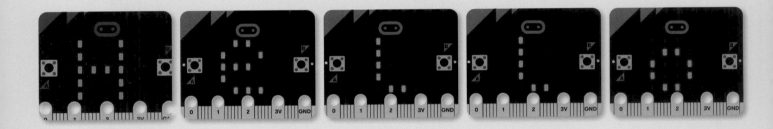

IN THIS SKILL SET

1. Display an icon

2. Create and display your own image

3. Pause the display

4. Clearing the screen

5. Make a name badge

LED stands for light-emitting diode.

1 Display an icon

Choose and display a
simple icon on the LED grid.

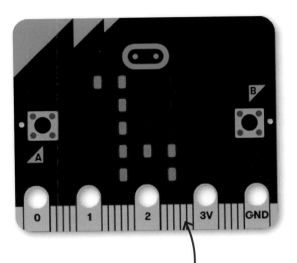

SKILLS YOU'LL LEARN

- Select an icon
- Display an icon

Can you guess
what it is?

GET YOUR BLOCKS

on start

show icon ▼

PUT IT TOGETHER

Drag the
show icon
block here.

on start

show icon ▼

on start

show icon ▼

Click the
drop-down
arrow to
select a
different
icon.

giraffe

THEORY

The micro:bit has
a set of pre-made
images called *icons*.

You can choose
different icons
to display on
the micro:bit
LED grid.

27

2 Create and display your own image

Make a custom image and display it on the LED grid.

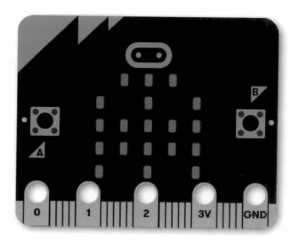

SKILLS YOU'LL LEARN

- Create and display an image
- Use the LED grid

GET YOUR BLOCKS

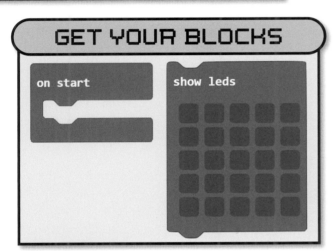

on start

show leds

It's really easy to design your own image.

PUT IT TOGETHER

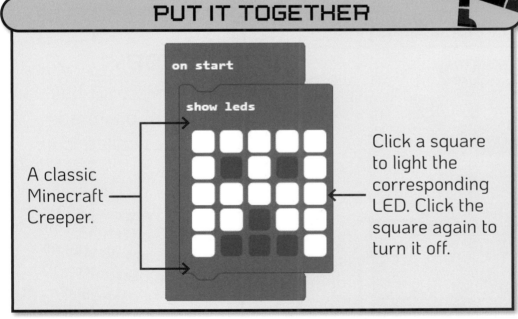

on start

show leds

A classic Minecraft Creeper.

Click a square to light the corresponding LED. Click the square again to turn it off.

THEORY

Each square represents one LED. By turning the LEDs on or off, you can create a custom image.

Try this image!

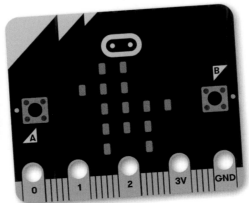

It looks like you, Smuffy!

3 Pause the display

Add pauses to your program to display a series of images for a certain length of time.

SKILLS YOU'LL LEARN

- Add a pause
- Change the length of the pause

GET YOUR BLOCKS

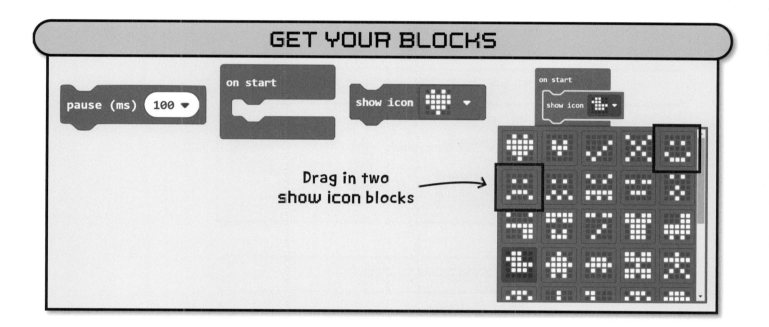

Drag in two show icon blocks

PUT IT TOGETHER

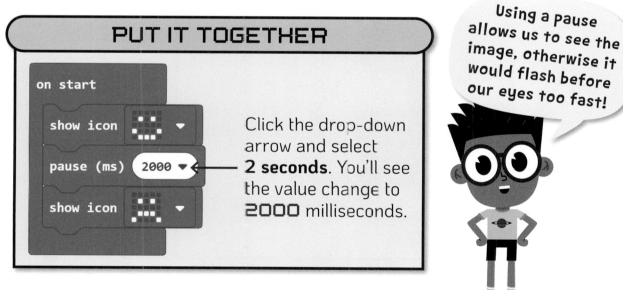

Click the drop-down arrow and select **2 seconds**. You'll see the value change to **2000** milliseconds.

Using a pause allows us to see the image, otherwise it would flash before our eyes too fast!

THEORY

You use pauses to freeze an action on the micro:bit for a certain length of time. The time is measured in milliseconds, so a value of 2000 ms (millisecords) displays the image for 2 seconds.

4 Clearing the screen

Removing the images from the LED grid.

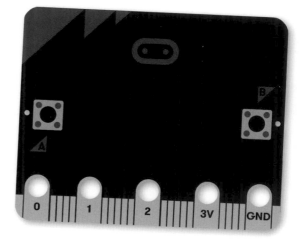

SKILLS YOU'LL LEARN

- Clear the LED grid
- Use the **forever** block

GET YOUR BLOCKS

forever

pause (ms) 100 ▼

clear screen

show icon ▼

PUT IT TOGETHER

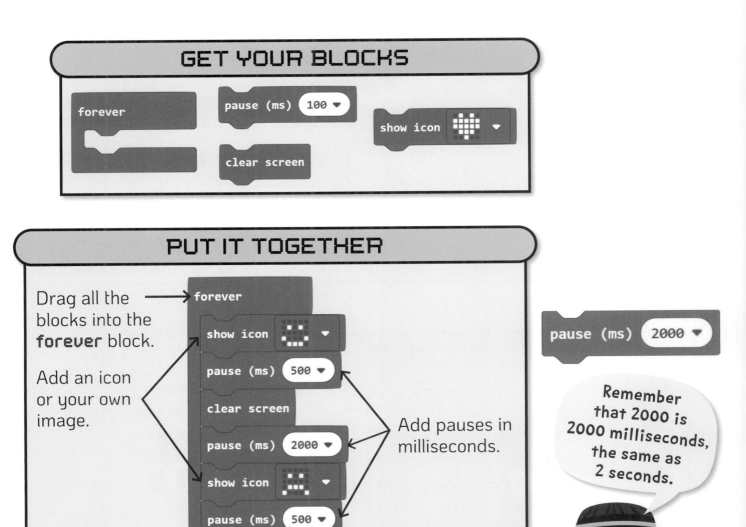

Drag all the blocks into the **forever** block.

Add an icon or your own image.

forever
show icon ▼
pause (ms) 500 ▼
clear screen
pause (ms) 2000 ▼
show icon ▼
pause (ms) 500 ▼

Add pauses in milliseconds.

pause (ms) 2000 ▼

Remember that 2000 is 2000 milliseconds, the same as 2 seconds.

THEORY

The **forever** block repeatedly runs the code inside it. The **clear screen** block turns all the LEDs off.

5 Make a name badge

Combine the skills from the previous pages to create a simple name badge.

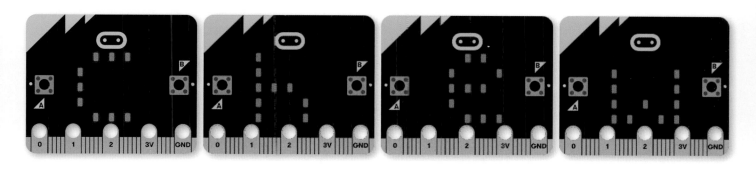

GET YOUR BLOCKS

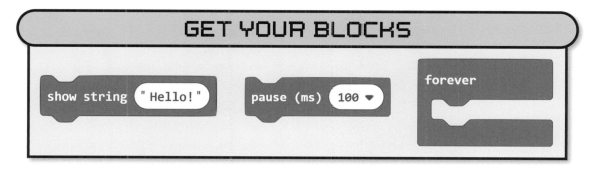

show string "Hello!"

pause (ms) 100 ▼

forever

PUT IT TOGETHER

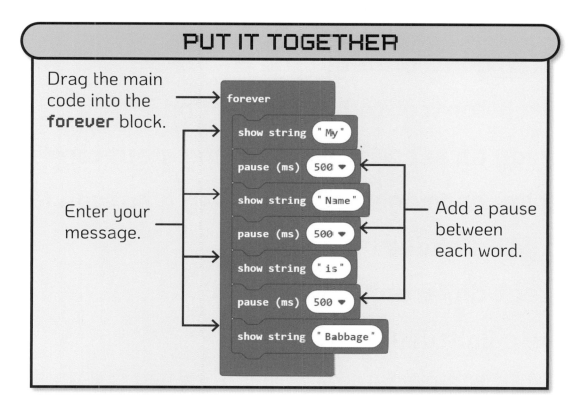

Drag the main code into the **forever** block.

Enter your message.

Add a pause between each word.

forever

show string " My "

pause (ms) 500 ▼

show string " Name "

pause (ms) 500 ▼

show string " is "

pause (ms) 500 ▼

show string " Babbage "

THEORY

The pause provides a short delay so you can read each word in your message as it scrolls by.

Try to code my name if you can!

Chew-Chew

31

SKILL SET 3
Inputs

Learn how to use the micro:bit buttons, known as *inputs*.

The buttons are clearly marked as A and B on your micro:bit.

IN THIS SKILL SET

1. Scroll a message by pressing a button
2. Switch control to button B
3. Switch control to buttons A and B
4. Display an image while pressing a button (1)
5. Display an image while pressing a button (2)
6. Detect a shake
7. Detect different movements
8. Take a light-level reading
9. Display a light-level reading
10. Respond to light-level readings (1)
11. Respond to light-level readings (2)

1 Scroll a message by pressing a button

Press button A to scroll a message across the LED grid.

SKILLS YOU'LL LEARN

- Trigger an event when you press a button

GET YOUR BLOCKS

> You'll explore using blocks from the Input group.

PUT IT TOGETHER

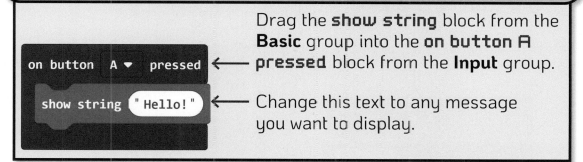

Drag the **show string** block from the **Basic** group into the **on button A pressed** block from the **Input** group.

Change this text to any message you want to display.

THEORY

You use an input any time you interact with the micro:bit to get it to do something. Here, the input is the button press.

TRY THIS

- Change **Hello!** to show a string of your choice
- Write the code to your micro:bit

2 Switch control to button B

Press button **B** to scroll a message across the LED grid.

SKILLS YOU'LL LEARN

- Move the code for button A to button B

GET YOUR BLOCKS

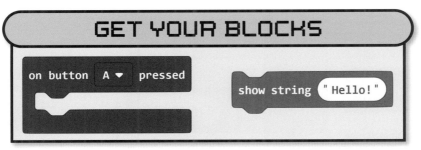

```
on button  A ▼  pressed

show string  "Hello!"
```

PUT IT TOGETHER

Drag the **on button A pressed** block from the **Input** group, and drag the **show string** block from the **Basic** group.

Click the arrow to change the button from **A** to **B**.

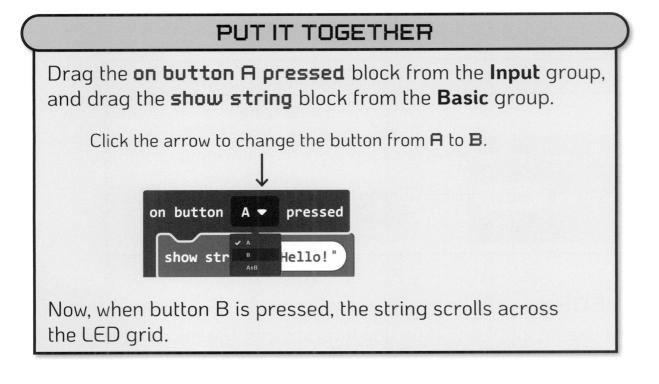

```
on button  A ▼  pressed
    ✓ A
show str  B    Hello!"
         A+B
```

Now, when button B is pressed, the string scrolls across the LED grid.

TRY THIS

- Replace the text with an image
- Change **Hello!** to show a string of your choice
- Write the code to your micro:bit

3 Switch control to buttons A and B together

Press buttons **A** and **B** at the same time to trigger an action.

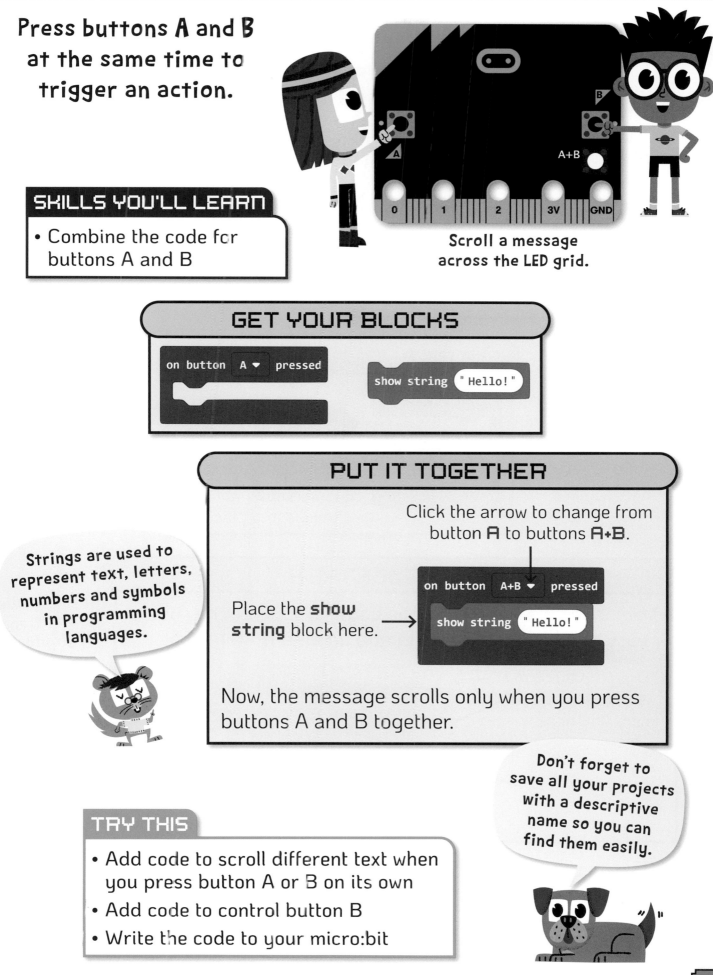

Scroll a message across the LED grid.

SKILLS YOU'LL LEARN

- Combine the code for buttons A and B

GET YOUR BLOCKS

on button A ▼ pressed

show string "Hello!"

PUT IT TOGETHER

Click the arrow to change from button **A** to buttons **A+B**.

Strings are used to represent text, letters, numbers and symbols in programming languages.

Place the **show string** block here. →

on button A+B ▼ pressed

show string "Hello!"

Now, the message scrolls only when you press buttons A and B together.

Don't forget to save all your projects with a descriptive name so you can find them easily.

TRY THIS

- Add code to scroll different text when you press button A or B on its own
- Add code to control button B
- Write the code to your micro:bit

4 Display an image while pressing a button (1)

Show a different icon while a button is being pressed.

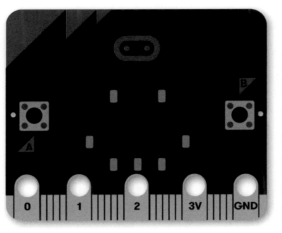

Press either button **A** or **B** to display an icon (or a message if you prefer). When you release the button, the display stops.

SKILLS YOU'LL LEARN

• Use **if**, **else if**, and **else** statements

GET YOUR BLOCKS

if true ▼ then

else   ⊖

⊕

button A ▼ is pressed

Drag the pink block into **true** until it clicks into place.

PUT IT TOGETHER

Drag an **if else** block from the **Logic** group into the coding area. Click the plus sign (**+**) to add an **else if** statement.

This is a called a conditional logic block.

Drag the **button A is pressed** block here and here.

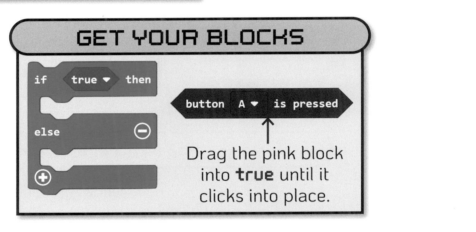

if button A ▼ is pressed then

else if button B ▼ is pressed then ⊖

else   ⊖

⊕

Change **A** to **B**.

THEORY

The **if**, **else if**, **else** block tells the micro:bit to do one thing while the button is being pressed and something else when it's not. As soon as you let go of the button, the **else** code runs, ending the action.

5 Display an image while pressing a button (2)

Add the blocks to display an icon and clear the LED grid when the button is released.

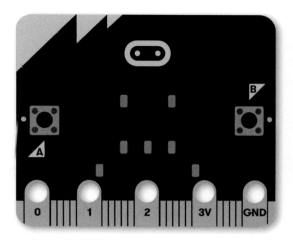

SKILLS YOU'LL LEARN

- Use a **forever** loop
- Add the **clear screen** block

GET YOUR BLOCKS

forever · clear screen · show icon

PUT IT TOGETHER

Put your entire **if**, **else if**, **else** block from the previous page inside the **forever** block.

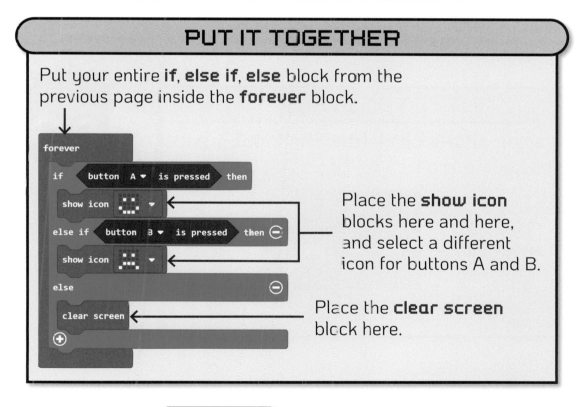

Place the **show icon** blocks here and here, and select a different icon for buttons A and B.

Place the **clear screen** block here.

TRY THIS

- Replace the icons with text
- Add an additional **else if** block to program a response to buttons A and B being pressed together

6 Detect a shake

Use the accelerometer to respond to the shaking of the micro:bit.

SKILLS YOU'LL LEARN

• Perform an action when the micro:bit is shaken

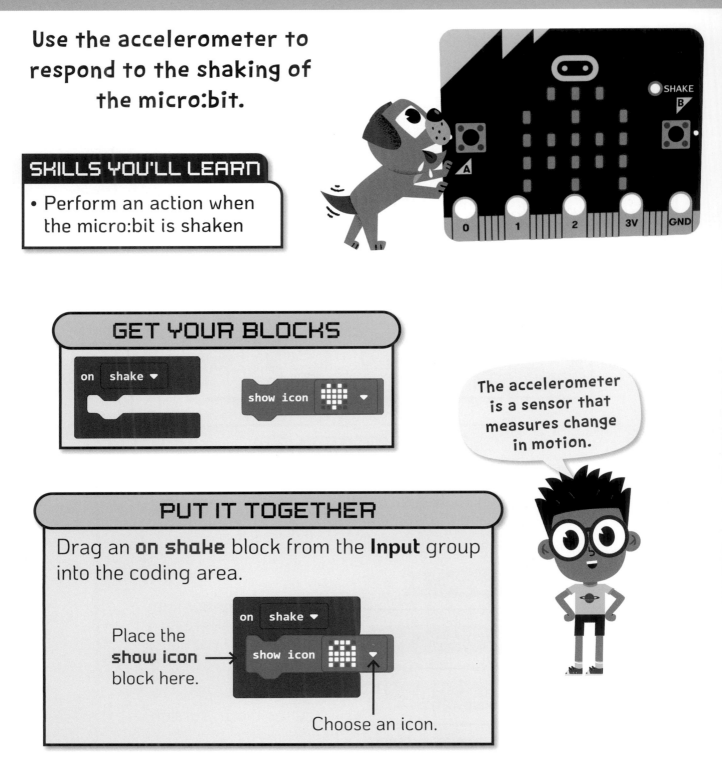

GET YOUR BLOCKS

on shake ▼

show icon ▼

The accelerometer is a sensor that measures change in motion.

PUT IT TOGETHER

Drag an **on shake** block from the **Input** group into the coding area.

on shake ▼

show icon

Place the **show icon** block here.

Choose an icon.

THEORY

The accelerometer detects when the micro:bit is shaken and responds with an action you define (in this case, displaying an icon). You can use the simulator to test the program, but it's best to download the program, add the battery pack, and try it out. Press the **Reset** button to enable the shake feature again.

7 Detect different movements

Track the position and motion of the micro:bit.

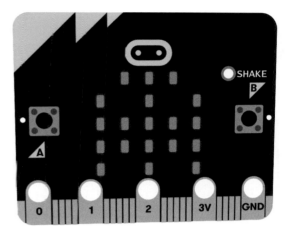

SKILLS YOU'LL LEARN

- Program the accelerometer to respond to different movements of the micro:bit

GET YOUR BLOCKS

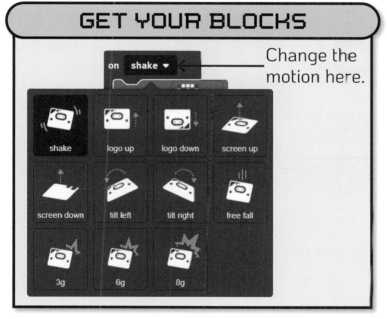

Change the motion here.

Screen down

Can you think of any other types of motion to try?

TRY THIS

The micro:bit can respond to different movements and gestures. Replace the **on shake** and try these:

MOTION TYPE	DETECTS WHEN...
logo up	...the micro:bit logo is facing upward
logo down	...the micro:bit logo is facing downward
screen up	...the micro:bit LEDs are facing upward
screen down	...the micro:bit LEDs are facing downward
tilt left	...the micro:bit is tilted to the left
tilt right	...the micro:bit is tilted to the right
free fall	...the micro:bit is dropped

8 Take a light-level reading

Take a reading of how much light is in the environment, where 0 is darkness and 255 is full daylight.

Maximum light!

SKILLS YOU'LL LEARN

• Create a variable
• Take a light-level reading

GET YOUR BLOCKS

Variables

Make a Variable...

set   light ▼   to   0

light level

Each Variable block must be given a name.

PUT IT TOGETHER

From the **Variables** group, click **Make a Variable**, name the variable light, and click **Ok**. This automatically creates a new **set light to** block in the **Variables** group. Drag that block into the coding area.

Type the word 'light' and click Ok.

New variable name:

Ok ✔   Cancel ✕

set   light ▼   to   light level

Drag the **light level** block from the **Input** group here.

THEORY

Variables are locations in the micro:bit memory where data can be stored. You assign each variable a name, which can then be used to access the data. After creating a variable, you can use the data stored in it, set it to a specific value, or change its value.

In this example, the **light level** block allows you to take a reading of the amount of light on the micro:bit. The light value is stored in the **light** variable. At the moment the program doesn't do anything except store the value, so the blocks will be shaded out.

9 Display a light-level reading

Instruct LEDs to display
the light-level reading.

128

255, scrolling →

SKILLS YOU'LL LEARN

• Display the light-level reading

B

A

0   1   2   3V   GND

The LED display
on the micro:bit
acts as a light
sensor.

GET YOUR BLOCKS

show number 0

light ▾

on start

set light ▾ to light level

PUT IT TOGETHER

Drag an **on start** block and a **show number** block
from the **Basic** group into the coding area.

on start

set light ▾ to light level

show number light ▾

Drag the **light** variable
from the previous
lesson here.

THEORY

When the program starts, the **light** variable is set to the **light level**
reading. The micro:bit then displays the value of **light** on the LED
grid. Use the simulator or download the code to your micro:bit to
try it out. The default light level on the simulator is 128.

10 Respond to light-level readings (1)

Write a program that responds in real time to the light level. Start by setting a light level to check for.

SKILLS YOU'LL LEARN

• Set a required light level

GET YOUR BLOCKS

light ▼   0 < ▼ 0

This is a less than comparison Logic block.

PUT IT TOGETHER

Drag the **<** (less than) comparison block from the **Logic** group into the coding area.

Drag the **light** variable from the previous lessons here.

↓

light ▼ < ▼ 25

↑

Change this value to **25**.

THEORY

The value on the right is the light level we're checking for. If the micro:bit detects that the light is below this level, it will perform an action, which we'll add next. You may want to change the **25** to a value that is suitable for your environment.

11 Respond to light-level readings (2)

Next, add icons to display at different light levels.

SKILLS YOU'LL LEARN

- Use an **if** statement
- Trigger a response

GET YOUR BLOCKS

forever

if true then
else ⊖
⊕

show icon ▼

clear screen

Try different levels and icons to get different readings.

PUT IT TOGETHER

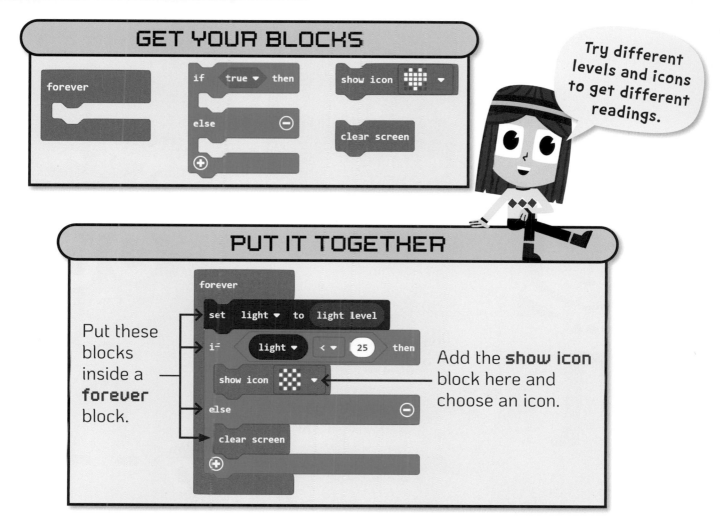

Put these blocks inside a **forever** block.

forever
  set light ▼ to light level
  if light ▼ < ▼ 25 then
    show icon ▼
  else ⊖
    clear screen
  ⊕

Add the **show icon** block here and choose an icon.

THEORY

The **if else** block checks if the light level is below **25** (or whatever value you set) and displays the icon if it is. If the light level is above the specified value, the **clear screen** block keeps the LED grid blank. The **forever** block keeps checking the light reading.

Project 1 >
The 99 game

In this game of chance, players stand in a circle and toss the micro:bit to each other. Each time someone throws the micro:bit it displays a random number. The player adds this number to a running total, starting from 0. When the total goes over 99, the player holding the micro:bit is eliminated, and the count resets to 0. The game continues until only one player remains.

Catch!

Don't let it go over 99!

Be careful when throwing the micro:bit!

SKILLS YOU'LL LEARN

- Create variables
- Select a random number
- Use the accelerometer

WHAT YOU'LL NEED

- Battery pack
- Two AAA batteries
- An elastic or rubber band

1 Create a variable

Get your blocks

Variables

Make a Variable...

Put it together

In the **Variables** menu, click **Make a Variable**. Name the new variable **number** and click **Ok**.

New variable name:

Ok ✔   Cancel ✘

Type the word 'number' here.

Theory

When you throw the micro:bit to another player, the program generates a random number and stores it in the **number** variable.

2 Select a random number

Get your blocks

pick random **0** to **10**   set number ▾ to **0**

Put it together

Drag the **set number to** block from the **Variables** group and the **pick random** block from the **Math** group into the coding area.

Drop the **pick random** block here.

set number ▾ to (pick random **0** to **10**)

Leave 0 and 10 as your range of numbers.

Theory

The program selects a random number between 0 and 10 and stores it in the **number** variable.

Setting a lower range, such as 0 to 5, would make the game last longer.

3 Show the number

Get your blocks

number ▾   show string "Hello!"

Put it together

Drag a **show string** block from the **Basic** group, and a **number** block from **Variables** into the coding area.

show string (number ▾) ← Add the **number** block here.

Theory

The program displays the count stored in the **number** variable on the LED grid so each player can see it before it's added to the total.

Shake it like a Polaroid picture!

4 Sense movement

Get your blocks

on shake ▾

Put it together

Drag the **on shake** block from the **Input** group into the coding area.

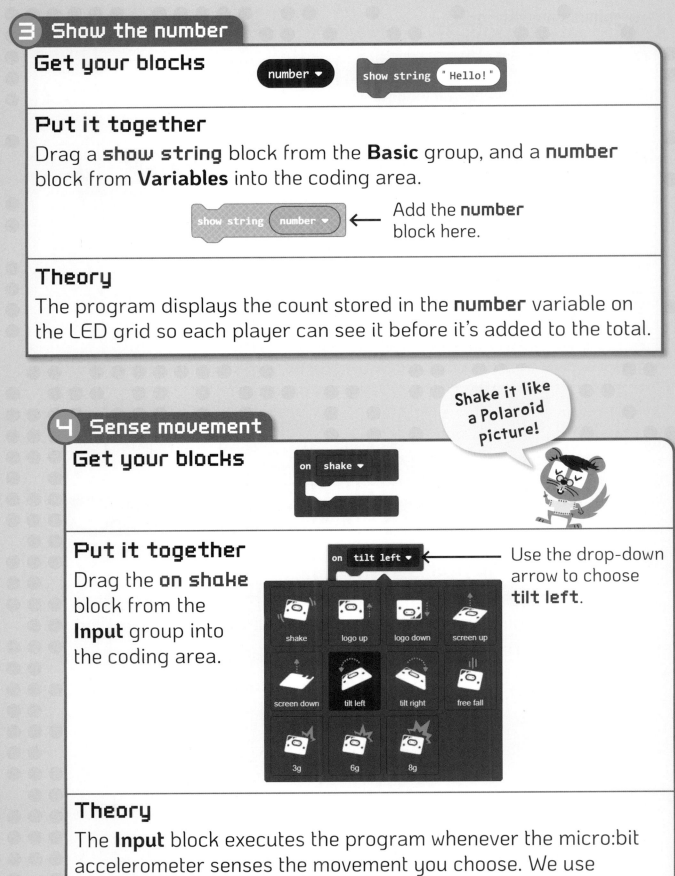

on tilt left ▾ ← Use the drop-down arrow to choose **tilt left**.

Theory

The **Input** block executes the program whenever the micro:bit accelerometer senses the movement you choose. We use **tilt left** so the micro:bit senses when it has been thrown and caught. You can change the movement to suit your gameplay style — for a gentle pass or a harder throw, for example.

5 Finish the code

Put it together

Add the **set number to** block here.

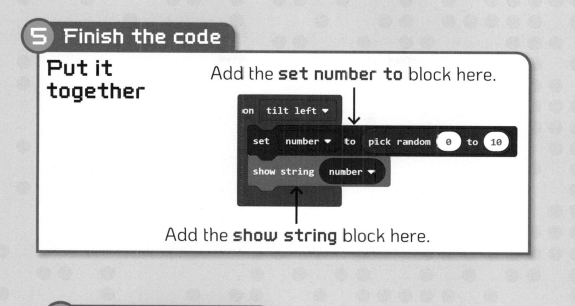

Add the **show string** block here.

6 Run the program

Download the code onto your micro:bit and add the battery pack. Use a small elastic band to secure the battery pack to the micro:bit.

Start the game!

To clear the display and start a new game, press the **Reset** button.

Remember to keep a running total!

7 Try this

Program your micro:bit so that it does one of the following:

- It starts at 99 and counts down, subtracting a random number each time.

- If you throw a 5, the micro:bit displays an X and the player misses a turn.

Heads or tails

Make a virtual coin-toss generator that displays heads, tails or void (to imitate you dropping the coin) when you throw the micro:bit into the air and catch it.

SKILLS YOU'LL LEARN

- Create variables
- Select a random number
- Use **if**, **else**, and **else if** statements

WHAT YOU'LL NEED

- Battery pack
- Two AAA batteries
- An elastic or rubber band

1 Create a variable

Get your blocks

Variables

Make a Variable...

pick random **0** to **10**

set outcome ▼ to **0**

Put it together

In the **Variables** group, click **Make a Variable**. Enter **outcome** as the name and click **Ok**. Drag the **set outcome to** block from the **Variables** group and the **pick random** block from the **Math** group into the coding area.

New variable name:

Ok ✔   Cancel ✗

set outcome ▼ to pick random **0** to **2**

Drop the **pick random** block here.   Change this value to **2**.

Theory

The **outcome** variable stores the outcome of the coin toss. A value of **0** represents heads, **1** represents tails, and **2** represents a void toss (for example, if the coin was dropped).

2 Use logic to determine results

Get your blocks

if true ▼ then

else ⊖

⊕

outcome ▼ = ▼ **0**

The **outcome** block can be found in the **Variables** menu.

Put it together

Drag the **if else block** from the **Input** group. Click **+** to add the **else if** statement.

Add two **comparison** blocks from the **Logic** group as shown.

Drop your **outcome** variables here and here.

set outcome ▼ to pick random **0** to **2**

if outcome ▼ = ▼ **0** then

else if outcome ▼ = ▼ **1** then ⊖

else ⊖

⊕

Change this to **1**.

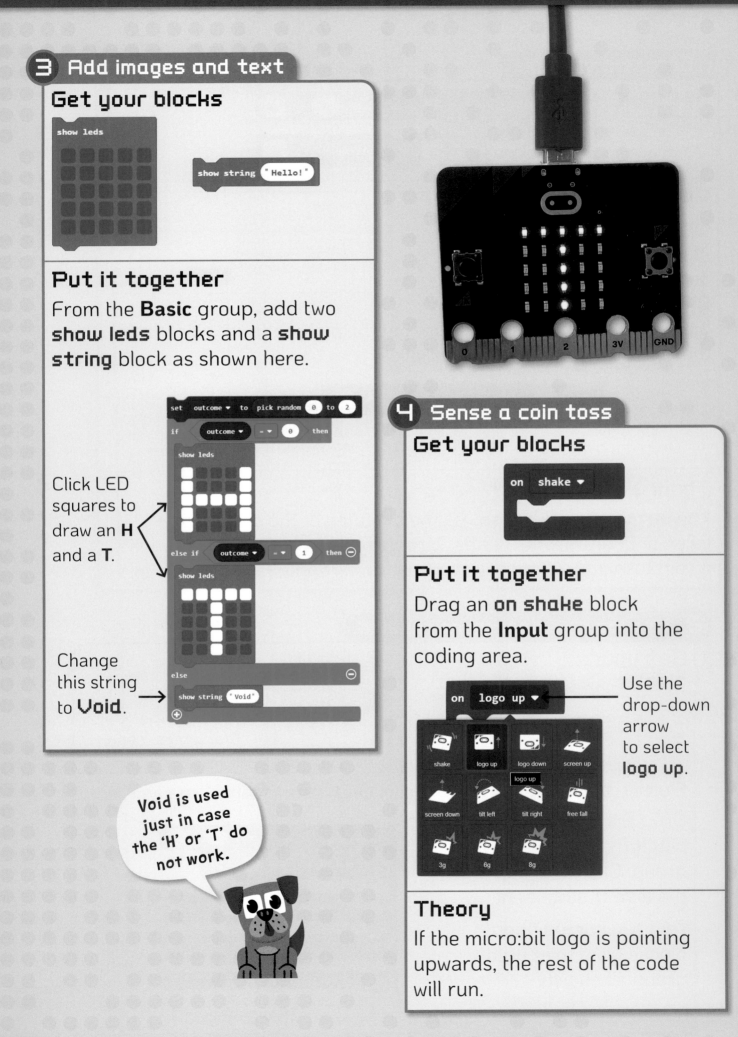

3 Add images and text

Get your blocks

show leds

show string "Hello!"

Put it together

From the **Basic** group, add two **show leds** blocks and a **show string** block as shown here.

set outcome ▼ to pick random 0 to 2

if outcome ▼ = ▼ 0 then

show leds

Click LED squares to draw an **H** and a **T**.

else if outcome ▼ = ▼ 1 then ⊖

show leds

Change this string to **Void**.

else ⊖

show string "Void"

⊕

Void is used just in case the 'H' or 'T' do not work.

4 Sense a coin toss

Get your blocks

on shake ▼

Put it together

Drag an **on shake** block from the **Input** group into the coding area.

on logo up ▼

shake · logo up · logo down · screen up

logo up

screen down · tilt left · tilt right · free fall

3g · 6g · 8g

Use the drop-down arrow to select **logo up**.

Theory

If the micro:bit logo is pointing upwards, the rest of the code will run.

5 Finish the code

Wrap the **on logo up** block around the rest of the blocks so that every time the micro:bit logo is facing upwards, the program runs.

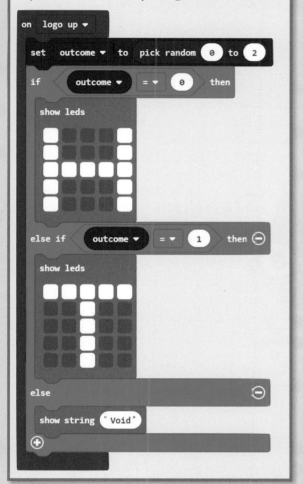

Download and let's play Heads or Tails!

6 Run the program

Download the code onto the micro:bit. Add the battery pack — use a small elastic band to secure it to the micro:bit.

Run the program. Throw the micro:bit up into the air and catch it. Watch as the display shows the corresponding image for heads, tails or void!

To clear the display, press the **Reset** button.

You could use different letters, such as U and D (Up and Down) or two different images.

Project 3 >
Steady hand game

How steady is your hand? Build a game to measure how long you can hold your micro:bit still before it senses you wobble. Challenge your friends and family to see who is the steadiest.

Steady!

Try not to wobble!

SKILLS YOU'LL LEARN

- Use the **acceleration** block
- Create variables
- Use **if else** statements

WHAT YOU'LL NEED

- Battery pack
- Two AAA batteries

1 Create a variable

Get your blocks

Make a Variable...

Put it together

Click **Make a Variable**. Name the variable **steady** and click **Ok**.

New variable name:

Ok ✔   Cancel ✕

Theory

Acceleration is a change in speed — either an increase or a decrease — in a particular direction. The micro:bit can sense up and down, left and right, and forward and backward motion using its built-in accelerometer. The accelerometer measures these changes and records the results as values. We use these values in program code to trigger events.

2 Store the acceleration value

Get your blocks

set steady ▼ to 0   acceleration (mg) x ▼

Put it together

Combine the **set steady to** block from the **Variables** group and the **acceleration** block from the **Input** group.

set steady ▼ to acceleration (mg) x ▼ ——— Replace the **0** with the **acceleration** block.

Theory

The accelerometer reads the acceleration of the micro:bit in the x-direction and saves the value in the **steady** variable.

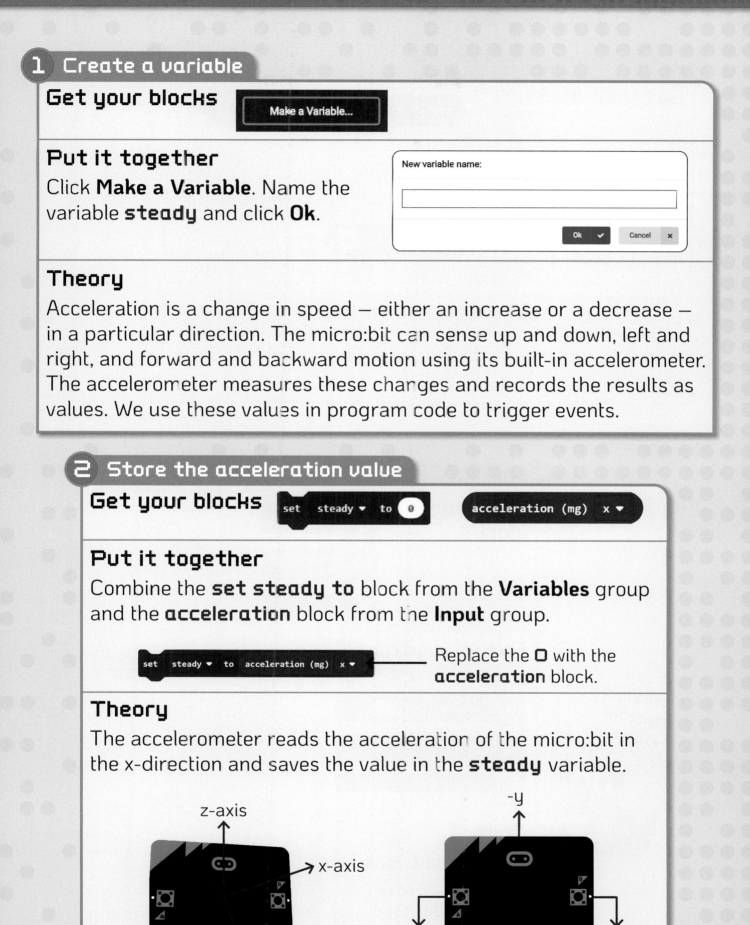

z-axis

x-axis

y-axis

-y

-x   +x

+y

3 Set a comparison value

Get your blocks

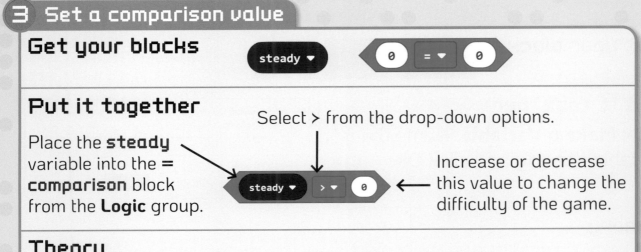

Put it together

Select > from the drop-down options.

Place the **steady** variable into the = **comparison** block from the **Logic** group.

Increase or decrease this value to change the difficulty of the game.

Theory

The **comparison** block checks if the acceleration value is greater than 0 (or whatever value you set). The higher the acceleration value, the easier the game.

4 Compare the values

Get your blocks

Put it together

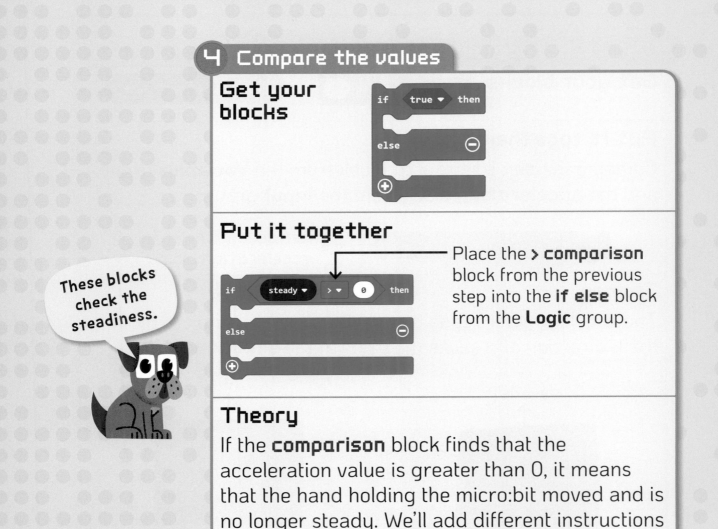

Place the **>** **comparison** block from the previous step into the **if else** block from the **Logic** group.

These blocks check the steadiness.

Theory

If the **comparison** block finds that the acceleration value is greater than 0, it means that the hand holding the micro:bit moved and is no longer steady. We'll add different instructions for staying steady and for wobbling.

5 Respond to winning or losing

Get your blocks

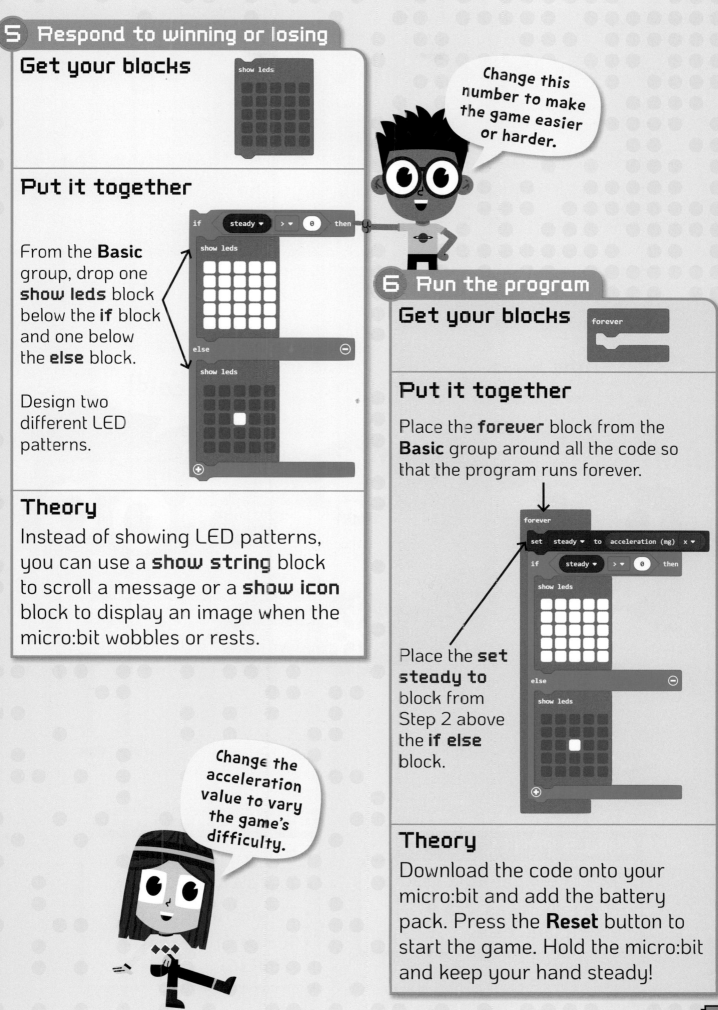

Put it together

From the **Basic** group, drop one **show leds** block below the **if** block and one below the **else** block.

Design two different LED patterns.

> Change this number to make the game easier or harder.

Theory

Instead of showing LED patterns, you can use a **show string** block to scroll a message or a **show icon** block to display an image when the micro:bit wobbles or rests.

> Change the acceleration value to vary the game's difficulty.

6 Run the program

Get your blocks

Put it together

Place the **forever** block from the **Basic** group around all the code so that the program runs forever.

Place the **set steady to** block from Step 2 above the **if else** block.

Theory

Download the code onto your micro:bit and add the battery pack. Press the **Reset** button to start the game. Hold the micro:bit and keep your hand steady!

Project 4 >
Temperature display

Build a real-time temperature monitor that senses the current temperature and displays the reading and a response on the micro:bit's LEDs.

SKILLS YOU'LL LEARN

- Take a temperature reading
- Make decisions with **if**, **else if**, and **else**

WHAT YOU'LL NEED

- Battery pack
- Two AAA batteries
- Three crocodile clips
- Temperature sensor (TMP36)

1 Wire up the temperature sensor

Connect one crocodile clip to each leg of the temperature sensor. With the flat face of the sensor facing you, attach the left wire to 3V, the middle wire to pin 0, and the right wire to GND. Separate the sensor's three legs to make sure the clips don't touch one another.

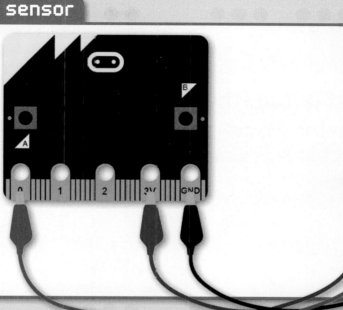

2 Test the set-up and sensor

Get your blocks

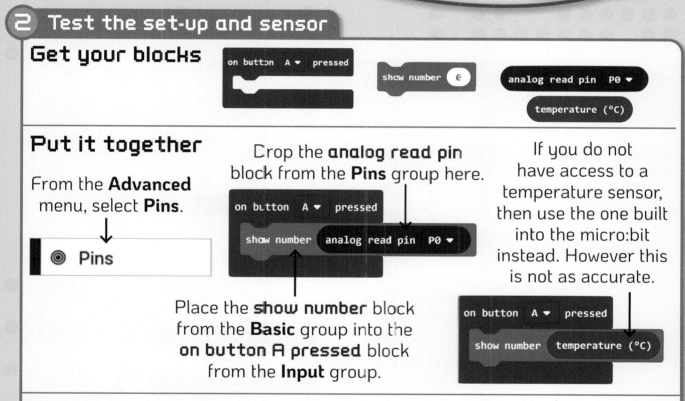

on button A ▾ pressed

show number 0

analog read pin P0 ▾

temperature (°C)

Put it together

From the **Advanced** menu, select **Pins**.

◉ Pins

Crop the **analog read pin** block from the **Pins** group here.

on button A ▾ pressed
show number analog read pin P0 ▾

Place the **show number** block from the **Basic** group into the **on button A pressed** block from the **Input** group.

If you do not have access to a temperature sensor, then use the one built into the micro:bit instead. However this is not as accurate.

on button A ▾ pressed
show number temperature (°C)

Try this

Download the program to test that you've wired the sensor correctly and that the program works. Connect the micro:bit to your computer with the USB cable. Then save and move the *.hex* file from your *Downloads* folder to the micro:bit.

Press button **A** to get a temperature reading in degrees Celsius and display it on the LEDs. There's no decimal point on the display, so a reading of 24.3 degrees, for example, will appear as 243.

3 Loop the program

Get your blocks

> If you are using the micro:bit's sensor then remember to replace the **analog read pin** block with the **temperature** block.

Put it together

Remove the **on button A pressed** block.

Place the **forever** block from the **Basic** group around all the code.

Combine the **show number** block with the **pause** block from the **Basic** group.

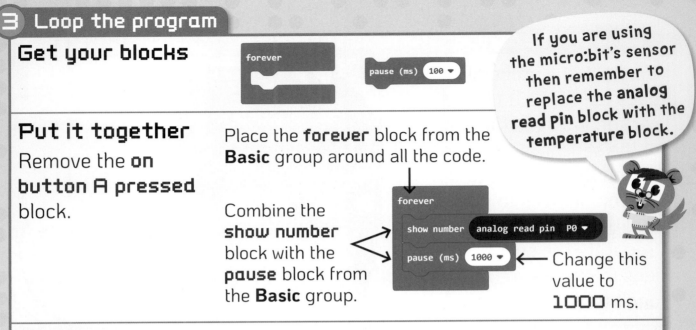

Change this value to **1000** ms.

Try this

The micro:bit now continually takes a temperature reading and displays it in real time, with a 1-second (1000-ms) pause between readings. Download the program and test it with the micro:bit. Try putting the sensor in the freezer to cool it down!

4 Compare the temperature readings

Get your blocks

Put it together

Drop an **analog read pin** block from the **Pins** group into the **comparison** blocks from the **Logic** group here and here.

Change the equal sign to **>**.

Change this value to **280**.

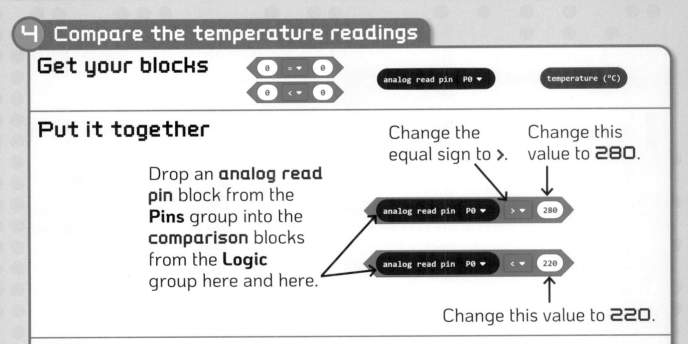

Change this value to **220**.

Theory

These blocks establish the higher and lower bounds of temperature; the micro:bit will respond if these limits are crossed. Change the temperature levels to suit your environment. You must use three numbers to represent the temperature — for example, 28 degrees is 280. Remember, the temperature is in degrees Celsius. See **Bonus Project: Convert to Fahrenheit** (p61) to use degrees Fahrenheit.

5 Respond to different temperatures

Get your blocks

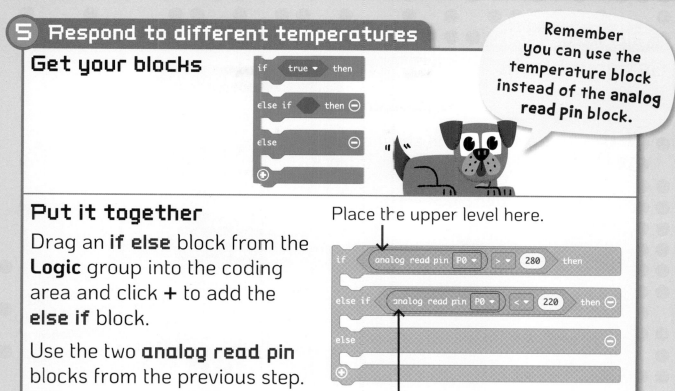

Remember you can use the **temperature block** instead of the **analog read pin block**.

Put it together

Drag an **if else** block from the **Logic** group into the coding area and click **+** to add the **else if** block.

Use the two **analog read pin** blocks from the previous step.

Place the upper level here.

Place the level here.

Theory

The **else if** block enables the program to respond differently to high and low temperatures. You'll need to change the values depending on your climate.

6 Add the responses

Get your blocks

You'll need three **show** blocks from the **Basic** group. They can be all the same kind or a combination. Show an LED shape you've created, display a pre-made icon, scroll a message, or do a mix of all three.

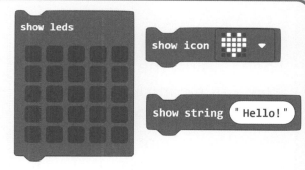

Put it together

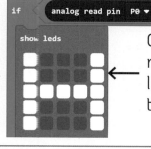

Create messages or icons that represent three temperature levels: too hot (shown here), too cold, and just right.

Theory

The program should display the message or icon corresponding to the current temperature level.

7 Finish the code

Get your blocks

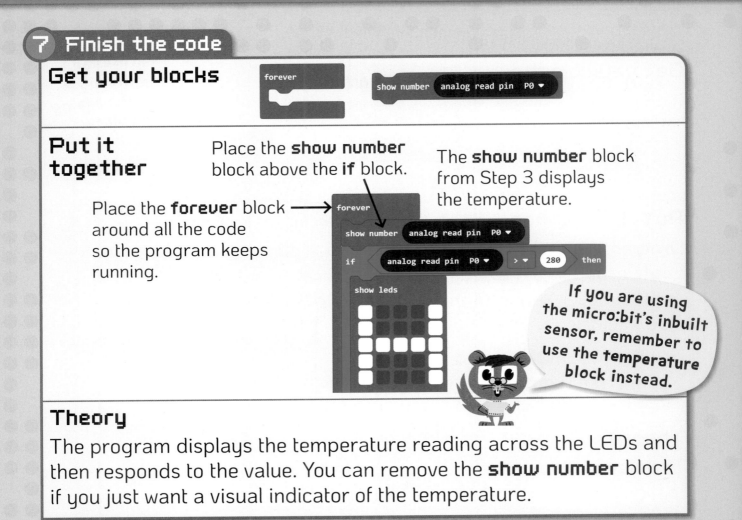

Put it together

Place the **forever** block around all the code so the program keeps running.

Place the **show number** block above the **if** block.

The **show number** block from Step 3 displays the temperature.

If you are using the micro:bit's inbuilt sensor, remember to use the temperature block instead.

Theory

The program displays the temperature reading across the LEDs and then responds to the value. You can remove the **show number** block if you just want a visual indicator of the temperature.

8 Run the program

Put it together

Download the program code to your micro:bit. Then unplug the micro:bit from your computer and add the battery pack. Place the sensor in a safe location, or in the fridge to lower the temperature, and watch the micro:bit respond.

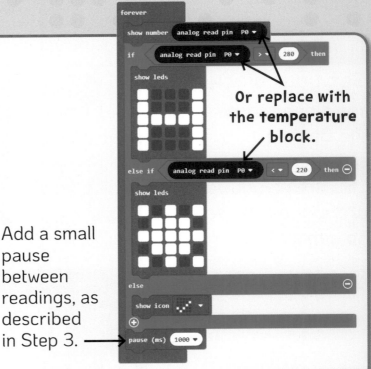

Or replace with the **temperature** block.

Add a small pause between readings, as described in Step 3.

Try this

Add more **else if** statements in Step 5 to extend the range of temperatures that the micro:bit responds to. For example, have five levels to indicate 'very cold', 'mildly cold', 'just right', 'mildly hot', and 'very hot'.

BONUS! Convert to Fahrenheit

Convert the micro:bit readings from Celsius to Fahrenheit.

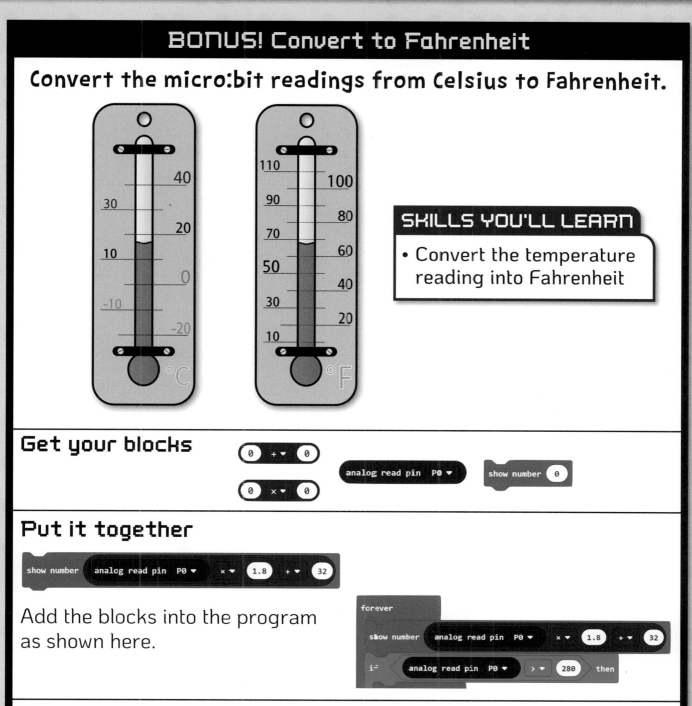

SKILLS YOU'LL LEARN

• Convert the temperature reading into Fahrenheit

Get your blocks

Put it together

Add the blocks into the program as shown here.

Theory

To convert the temperature, multiply the Celsius value by 1.8 and then add 32. For example:

- 0°C = (0 × 1.8) + 32 = 32°F
- 5°C = (5 × 1.8) + 32 = 41°F
- 10°C = (10 × 1.8) + 32 = 50°F

Use these blocks to create a temperature sensor that responds to Fahrenheit values. Simply replace the **show number** block with the **Fahrenheit calculation** block. You don't need to change the values in the **if** and **else if** blocks.

Project 5 >
LED control

Discover how to wire an LED to the micro:bit. Then learn how to use code to turn the LED on, turn it off, and even make it flash.

I want white.

I like red.

SKILLS YOU'LL LEARN

- Wire an LED
- Use buttons to control an LED
- Make an LED blink

WHAT YOU'LL NEED

- Battery pack
- Two AAA batteries
- Two crocodile clips with wires
- An LED

1 Wire the LED

Connect a crocodile clip wire to the longer LED leg; this is the positive leg. Connect a clip wire to the shorter (negative) LED leg. Attach the wire of the positive leg to pin 2 and the wire of the negative leg to the GND pin.

Make sure that the clips do not touch each other.

2 Press button A to turn the LED on

Get your blocks

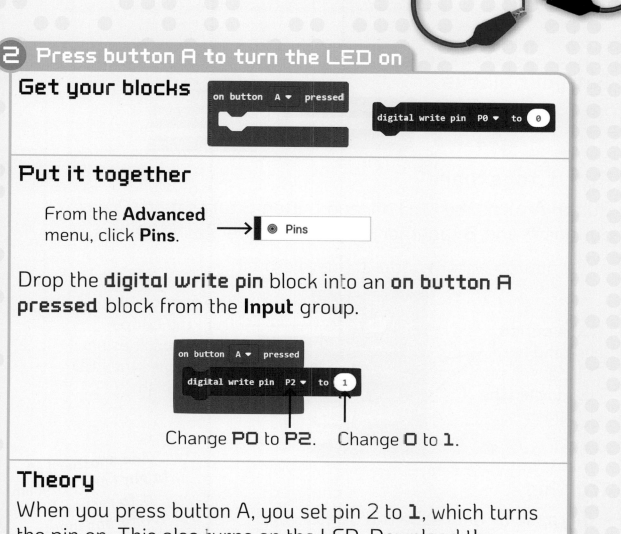

Put it together

From the **Advanced** menu, click **Pins**.

→ ◉ Pins

Drop the **digital write pin** block into an **on button A pressed** block from the **Input** group.

```
on button A ▼ pressed
    digital write pin P2 ▼ to 1
```

Change **P0** to **P2**.   Change **0** to **1**.

Theory

When you press button A, you set pin 2 to **1**, which turns the pin on. This also turns on the LED. Download the program and test that it is working correctly.

3 Press button B to turn the LED off

Get your blocks

`digital write pin P0 ▾ to 0`

`on button A ▾ pressed`

Put it together

Change A to **B**.

Keep this set at **0**.

`on button B ▾ pressed`
`digital write pin P2 ▾ to 0`

Change P0 to **P2**.

Theory

When you press button B, you set pin 2 to **0**, which turns that pin off, also turning off the LED. Download the program and test that it is working correctly.

4 Run the program

Get your blocks

`repeat 10 times do`

`digital write pin P2 ▾ to 0`

`digital write pin P2 ▾ to 1`

`pause (ms) 1000 ▾`

`on button A+B ▾ pressed`

Put it together

Button A turns the LED on, and button B turns it off. Press buttons **A** and **B** together to make the LED flash 10 times.

Write your program code to the micro:bit.

Add a **pause** here and here. The pauses set how quickly the LED flashes.

`on button A+B ▾ pressed`
`repeat 10 times`
`do digital write pin P2 ▾ to 1`
`pause (ms) 1000 ▾`
`digital write pin P2 ▾ to 0`
`pause (ms) 1000 ▾`

The **repeat** block from the **Loops** group specifies how many times the LED should flash.

Add another LED to Pin 1 and program it to respond to different inputs.

Try this

- Increase or decrease the number of times the LED flashes.

- Add a different trigger — for example, a shake or tilt.

Project 6 >
Trespasser alarm

Build an alarm system that plays loud music when triggered, and rig it up to your bedroom door. You'll know when pesky people enter your room! Then go on to try out the bonus project and add a sound sensor (see page 70).

HOWWL!

SKILLS YOU'LL LEARN

- Use **Music** blocks
- Hack headphones
- Read inputs from a pin
- Use loops

WHAT YOU'LL NEED

- Battery pack
- Two AAA batteries
- A speaker or headphones
- Four crocodile clips
- Foil

1 Wire up your speaker or headphones

NOTE: If you're using the micro:bit V2, you can skip this step and use the built-in speaker. However, attaching an external speaker will make the alarm louder.

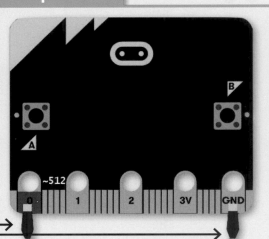

Clip one crocodile clip onto pin 0. Clip a second crocodile clip onto the GND pin.

Clip the GND wire to the base of your headphones' or speaker's audio jack. Clip the pin 0 wire to the tip of the audio jack.

WARNING:
The micro:bit has no volume control, so **do not** place your headphones/earbuds over/in your ears.

2 Play a note or melody

Get your blocks

```
play tone  Middle C  for  1 ▼  beat

start melody  dadadum ▼  repeating  once ▼

on button  A ▼  pressed
```

Put it together

Combine either the **play tone** or **start melody** block from the **Music** group with an **on button A pressed** block from the **Input** group.

Set the duration of the note.

Set the number of times the melody plays.

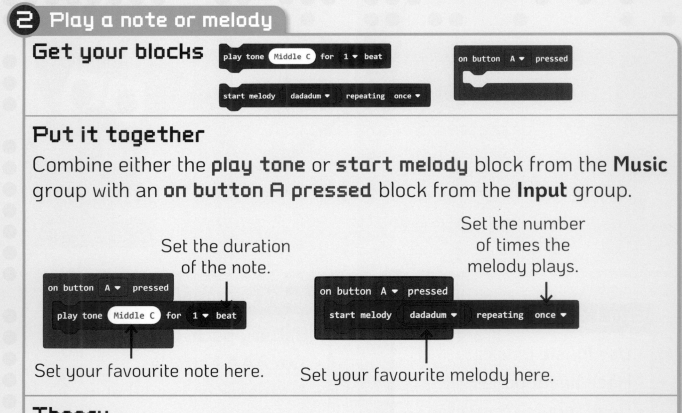

Set your favourite note here.

Set your favourite melody here.

Theory

The program checks if button A is being pressed. If it is, your chosen note plays for 1 second, or your chosen melody plays once.

3 Create an alarm trigger

Combine the micro:bit music with a speaker to create a musical alarm (headphones won't work for this experiment).

Connect a speaker to the micro:bit using the instructions in Step 1.

Clip a third crocodile clip to pin 1 and a fourth clip to the 3V pin, then clip them together to create a circuit. Once you download the code, the alarm should trigger when these two clips are disconnected.

An external speaker is required only if you are using the micro:bit V1 or want a louder alarm.

4 Check if the wires have been disconnected

Get your blocks

digital read pin P0 ▼   0 = ▼ 0

Put it together

From the **Advanced** menu, click the **Pins** group. Combine the **digital read pin** block with the = comparison block from the **Logic** group.

Change **P0** to **P1**.

digital read pin P1 ▼   = ▼ 1

Set the value to **1**.

Theory

The **digital read pin** block checks if pin 1 is connected to the 3V wire, which means that pin 1 is **true** and the circuit is still intact. The alarm should not sound as long as pin 1 is **true**.

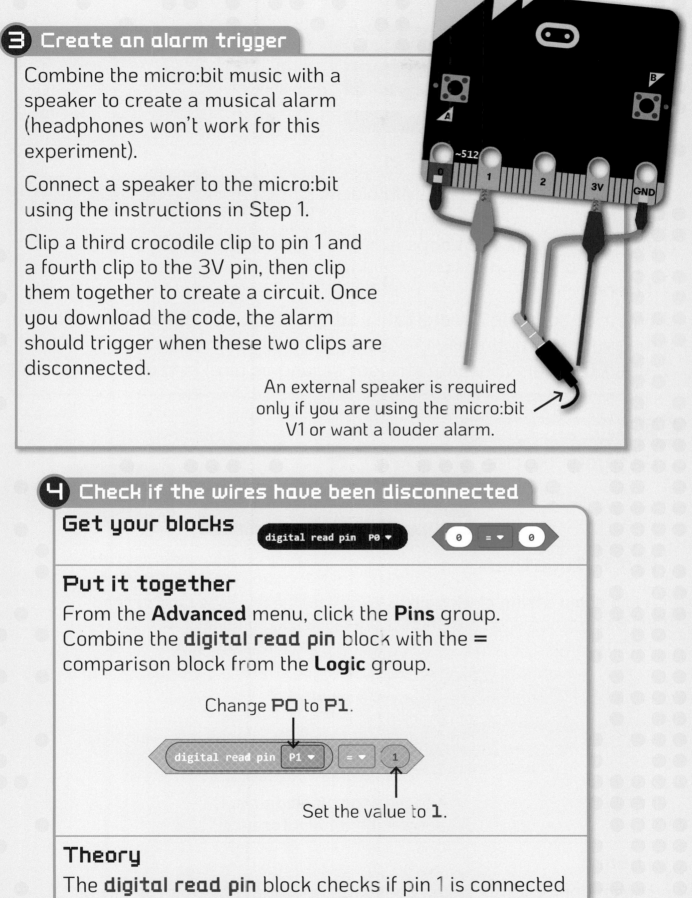

5 Continually check the alarm

Get your blocks

```
while  true ▾
do
```

Put it together

Combine the **digital read pin** block from the previous step with the **while** block from the **Loops** group.

```
while  ( digital read pin  P1 ▾ )  = ▾  1
do
```

Theory

When we combine the **digital read pin** block with the **while** block, the program continually checks if pin 1 is **true** and has a value of **1**. Again, the alarm shouldn't trigger as long as pin 1 is **true**.

6 Sound the alarm

Get your blocks

```
show string  " Hello! "
```

```
start melody  dadadum ▾  repeating  once ▾
```

```
if  true ▾  then
⊕
```

Put it together

Add a **show string** block from the **Basic** group and enter this alert message.

Duplicate the previous **digital read pin** block and combine it with the **if** block from the **Logic** group.

```
show string  " ALARM ACTIVE "
if  ( digital read pin  P1 ▾ )  = ▾  0   then
    start melody  ( dadadum ▾ )  repeating  forever ▾
⊕
```

Change this value to **0**.

Add the **start melody** block and set it to repeat **forever**.

Theory

These blocks display your message and then check if the circuit is connected. If a value of **1** is returned, the circuit is connected. If the value of pin 1 is **0** (off), it should trigger the alarm melody to play forever, until you reset the micro:bit.

7 Activate the alarm

Cut a length of foil long enough to reach across a door frame.

Clip the pin 1 crocodile clip to one end of the foil, and the 3V crocodile clip to the other end.

Place the foil across a door frame. When the door opens, the foil should tear, break the circuit, and trigger the alarm to sound over the speaker.

Place foil where the door meets the door frame

Door frame

8 Run the program

Put it together

Download the program to your micro:bit. When you clip the two crocodile clips together, the pin value is set at **1** and the micro:bit scrolls the message **ALARM ACTIVE**.

Unclip the two wires to trigger the alarm.

Try this

- Create your own alarm melody.

- Add a flashing LED display.

- Display a message when the alarm is triggered.

- Combine this program with **Radio** blocks to alert you remotely that the alarm has been triggered (Project 9 Radio communication p84).

- If you have a micro:bit V2, try the following Bonus project to add a sound sensor to your alarm.

BONUS! Add a sound sensor (micro:bit V2 only)

Use the built-in speaker and microphone in the micro:bit V2 to add a sound sensor to the trespasser alarm. You can program the sensor to listen for loud or quiet sounds (like from a snooping sibling or a naughty pet!).

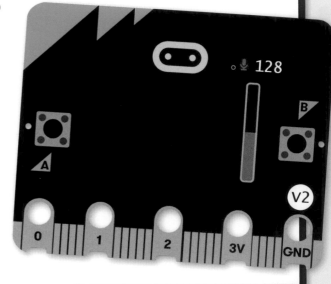

SKILLS YOU'LL LEARN

• Use the built-in speaker
• Use the built-in microphone

1 Play a sound through the built-in speaker

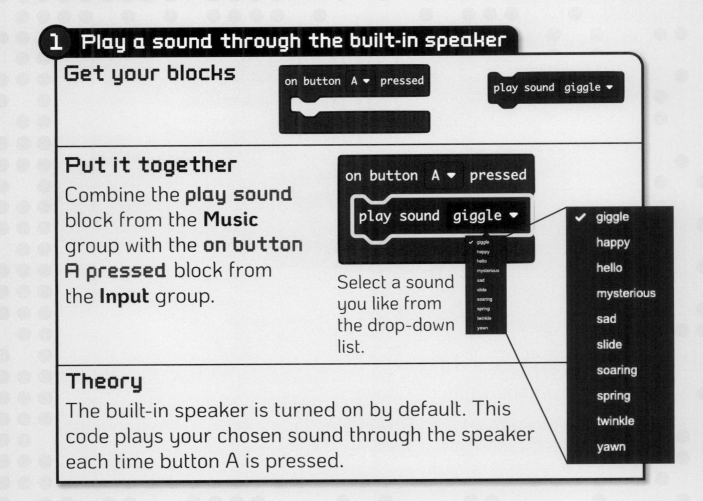

Get your blocks

Put it together

Combine the **play sound** block from the **Music** group with the **on button A pressed** block from the **Input** group.

Select a sound you like from the drop-down list.

Theory

The built-in speaker is turned on by default. This code plays your chosen sound through the speaker each time button A is pressed.

2 Turn off the built-in speaker

Get your blocks

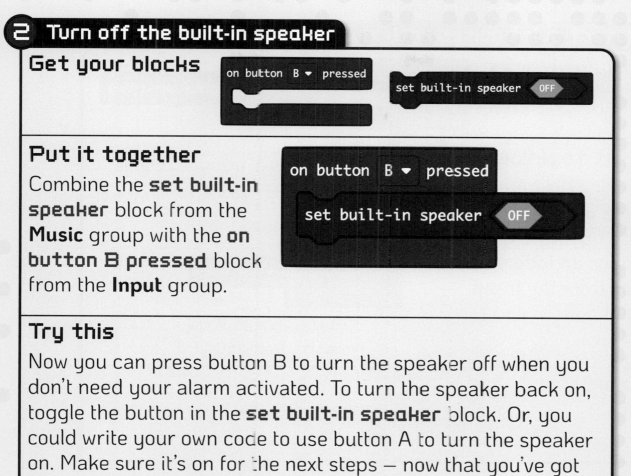

Put it together

Combine the **set built-in speaker** block from the **Music** group with the **on button B pressed** block from the **Input** group.

Try this

Now you can press button B to turn the speaker off when you don't need your alarm activated. To turn the speaker back on, toggle the button in the **set built-in speaker** block. Or, you could write your own code to use button A to turn the speaker on. Make sure it's on for the next steps — now that you've got the skills, it's time to put the alarm to work!

3 Detect loud noises with the microphone

Get your blocks

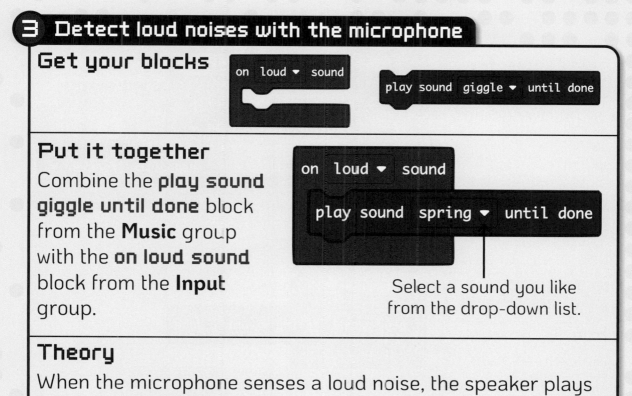

Put it together

Combine the **play sound giggle until done** block from the **Music** group with the **on loud sound** block from the **Input** group.

Select a sound you like from the drop-down list.

Theory

When the microphone senses a loud noise, the speaker plays the sound you chose.

4 Detect quiet noises with the microphone

Get your blocks

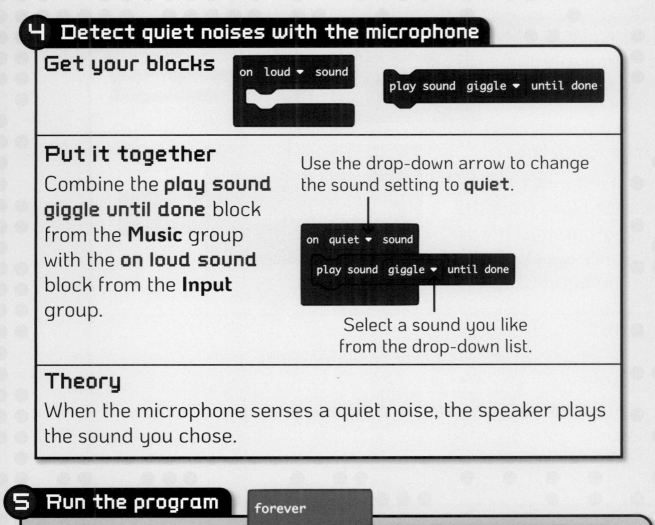

Put it together

Combine the **play sound giggle until done** block from the **Music** group with the **on loud sound** block from the **Input** group.

Use the drop-down arrow to change the sound setting to **quiet**.

Select a sound you like from the drop-down list.

Theory

When the microphone senses a quiet noise, the speaker plays the sound you chose.

5 Run the program

Combine the sound sensor code with the trespasser alarm code to create a more robust alarm system.

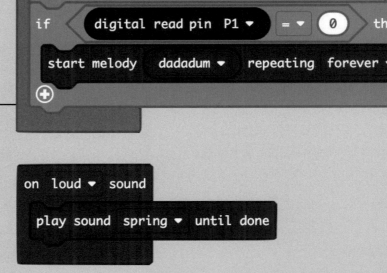

Try this

- Place the micro:bit into a drawer and get the alarm to trigger if someone opens the drawer.

- Turn the sound sensor into a game. Gather some friends and see who can stay silent the longest.

Project 7 >
Fortune teller

Ever wanted to predict the future? This project will show you how! Ask a question, shake the micro:bit, and watch the answer appear before your eyes.

Look into the crystal ball!

SKILLS YOU'LL LEARN

- Create an array (create a list and add text to it)
- Find the length of an array
- Select a random number based on the length of an array

WHAT YOU'LL NEED

- Battery pack
- Two AAA batteries

1 Create an array

Get your blocks

on start

set text list ▾ to array of "a" "b" "c" ⊖ ⊕

Put it together

In the **Advanced** menu, select **Arrays** and then select **set text list to array of**.

on start

set text list ▾ to array of "Yes" "No" "Maybe" ⊖ ⊕

Enter the response options here.

Theory

An *array* is used to hold several items at once. We store the future predictor's possible responses (**Yes**, **No**, and **Maybe**) in an array named **text list**. Click the plus symbol to add more responses.

2 Select a response

Get your blocks

Make a Variable...

response ▾

length of array list ▾

pick random 0 to 10

set response ▾ to 0

Put it together

Create a new variable called **response**.

Combine the **pick random** block from the **Math** group with the **length of array** block from the **Arrays** group.

set response ▾ to pick random 0 to length of array text list ▾

Change the **list** variable to **text list**.

Theory

The **pick random** block selects a number between 0 and the length of the array. For example, if the array contains 10 entries, **pick random** selects a random number between 0 and 10. This number is stored in the **response** variable.

3 Display the response part 1

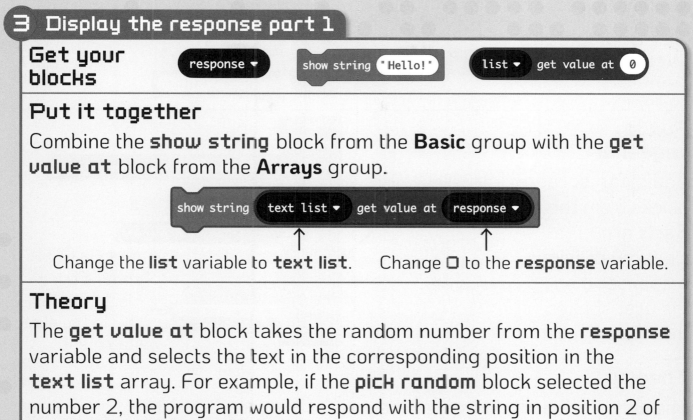

Get your blocks

response ▾   show string "Hello!"   list ▾ get value at 0

Put it together

Combine the **show string** block from the **Basic** group with the **get value at** block from the **Arrays** group.

show string text list ▾ get value at response ▾

Change the **list** variable to **text list**.   Change **0** to the **response** variable.

Theory

The **get value at** block takes the random number from the **response** variable and selects the text in the corresponding position in the **text list** array. For example, if the **pick random** block selected the number 2, the program would respond with the string in position 2 of the **text list** array: **Maybe**.

4 Display the response part 2

Get your blocks

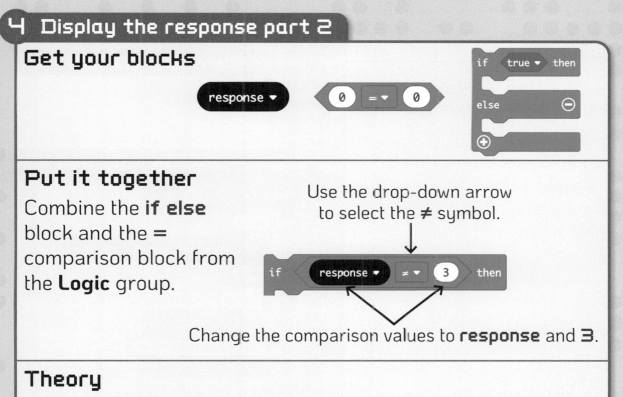

response ▾   0 = ▾ 0   if true ▾ then else ⊖ ⊕

Put it together

Combine the **if else** block and the **=** comparison block from the **Logic** group.

Use the drop-down arrow to select the ≠ symbol.

if response ▾ ≠ ▾ 3 then

Change the comparison values to **response** and **3**.

Theory

Sometimes the program will select a value outside of the array, which means that it won't have a response to return. The **if** statement checks for this error. We'll add code to handle this case in the next step.

5 Display the response part 3

Get your blocks

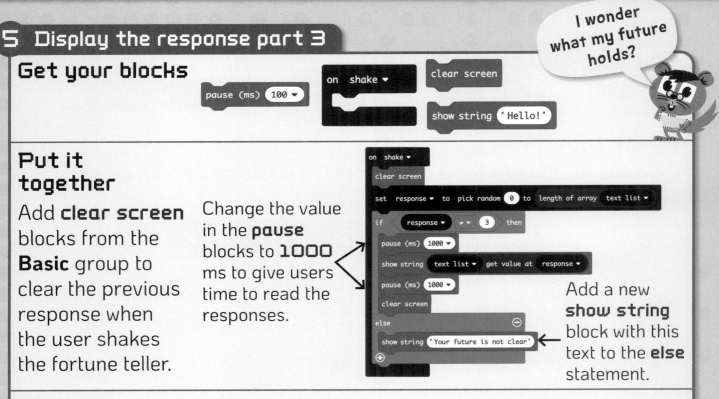

I wonder what my future holds?

pause (ms) 100 ▼

on shake ▼

clear screen

show string "Hello!"

Put it together

Add **clear screen** blocks from the **Basic** group to clear the previous response when the user shakes the fortune teller.

Change the value in the **pause** blocks to **1000** ms to give users time to read the responses.

```
on shake ▼
  clear screen
  set response ▼ to pick random 0 to length of array text list ▼
  if    response ▼ ≠ ▼ 3 then
    pause (ms) 1000 ▼
    show string text list ▼ get value at response ▼
    pause (ms) 1000 ▼
    clear screen
  else                                          ⊖
    show string "Your future is not clear"
  ⊕
```

Add a new **show string** block with this text to the **else** statement.

Theory

The **else** statement addresses the case of the program selecting a value outside of the array. Now, instead of getting no response, the user will see the message **Your future is not clear**.

6 Run the program

Download the program and add the battery pack. Ask your question out loud and shake the micro:bit. The LED grid should clear, and the program should select and display a random response. It then clears the LED grid again and waits for the next shake.

```
on start
  set text list ▼ to array of "Yes" "No" "Maybe" ⊖ ⊕
```

```
on shake ▼
  clear screen
  set response ▼ to pick random 0 to length of array text list ▼
  if    response ▼ ≠ ▼ 3 then
    pause (ms) 1000 ▼
    show string text list ▼ get value at response ▼
    pause (ms) 1000 ▼
    clear screen
  else                                          ⊖
    show string "Your future is not clear"
  ⊕
```

Try this

• Build a case for the future-predicting micro:bit or attach it to a cuddly toy.

• Add more responses — don't forget to change the response number.

• Use the **Music** blocks from Trespasser alarm project to add sound effects to the fortune teller.

• Add animations or images to make the fortune teller more fun.

Are you lost? Don't know which direction to go? Use the micro:bit's built-in magnetometer to build your own compass.

Let's navigate this together!

SKILLS YOU'LL LEARN

- Use the built-in magnetometer
- Calibrate the compass
- Take compass readings
- Use comparison blocks
- Display a compass direction

WHAT YOU'LL NEED

- Battery pack
- Two AAA batteries

1 Calibrate the compass

Get your blocks

on start

calibrate compass

> You should calibrate the compass from time to time.

Put it together

Combine the **on start** block with the **calibrate compass** block, which you can find in the **Input** group's **more** menu.

on start

calibrate compass

Theory

The micro:bit uses a *magnetometer*, an instrument that measures magnetic forces, to find North. The first time you use the micro:bit compass, you have to calibrate it so its readings will be accurate.

Download this program and rotate the micro:bit until all the LEDs are lit. When the micro:bit is calibrated, you'll see a smiley face on the screen.

2 Set the range for North

Get your blocks

0 < ▾ 0

compass heading (°)

Put it together

Insert the **compass heading** block from the **Input** group into the comparison block from the **Logic** group.

Use the drop-down arrow to select the ≥ symbol.

compass heading (°) ≥ ▾ 315

Change the lower limit value to **315**.

Duplicate the combined **compass heading** and comparison block.

Use the drop-down arrow to select the ≤ symbol.

compass heading (°) ≤ ▾ 360

Change the upper limit value to **360**.

Theory

The micro:bit uses the value in the **compass heading** block to find out if the micro:bit is pointing North, East, South or West. A **compass heading** value between 315° and 360° indicates North.

3 Combine the comparison blocks

Get your blocks

and ▾

Put it together

Drop the **and** block from the
Logic group into the coding area.

compass heading (°)   ≥ ▾   315   and ▾   compass heading (°)   ≤ ▾   360

Add the **315**
comparison block here.

Add the **360**
comparison block here.

Theory

The **and** block checks whether the micro:bit's current direction
is between 315° and 360° to see if it's facing northwards.

4 Respond to a North reading part 1

Get your blocks

compass heading (°)   ≥ ▾   315   and ▾   compass heading (°)   ≤ ▾   360

if   true ▾   then   forever

Put it together

Insert the combined **compass heading**
comparison block from the previous step
into the **if** block from the **Logic** group.

forever
if   compass heading (°)   ≥ ▾   315   and ▾   compass heading (°)   ≤ ▾   360   then

Insert the whole **if** block into the
forever block from the **Basic** group.

> Double-check
> you've got this
> long block of
> code correct.

Theory

The **if** block lets us specify some action to take if the
compass is between 315° and 360°. We'll light up certain
LEDs to indicate North in the next step.

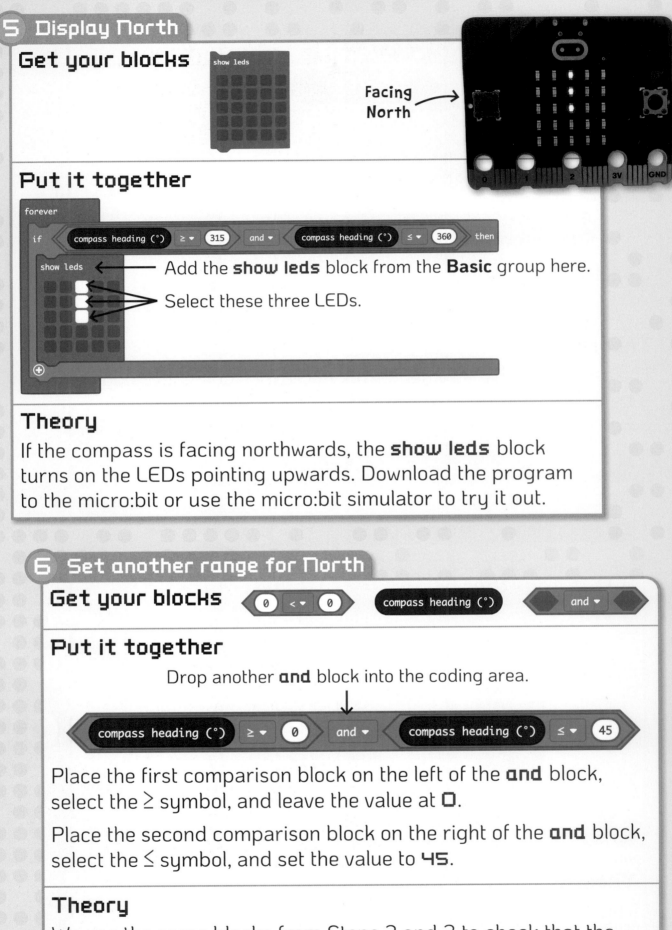

5 Display North

Get your blocks

show leds

Facing North

Put it together

forever

if compass heading (°) ≥ ▾ 315 and ▾ compass heading (°) ≤ ▾ 360 then

show leds ← Add the **show leds** block from the **Basic** group here.

Select these three LEDs.

Theory

If the compass is facing northwards, the **show leds** block turns on the LEDs pointing upwards. Download the program to the micro:bit or use the micro:bit simulator to try it out.

6 Set another range for North

Get your blocks

0 < ▾ 0   compass heading (°)   and ▾

Put it together

Drop another **and** block into the coding area.

compass heading (°) ≥ ▾ 0 and ▾ compass heading (°) ≤ ▾ 45

Place the first comparison block on the left of the **and** block, select the ≥ symbol, and leave the value at **0**.

Place the second comparison block on the right of the **and** block, select the ≤ symbol, and set the value to **45**.

Theory

We use the same blocks from Steps 2 and 3 to check that the **compass heading** value is between 0° and 45°. North also falls into this range.

7 Respond to a North reading part 2

Get your blocks

compass heading (°) ≥ ▾ 0 and ▾ compass heading (°) ≤ ▾ 45

show leds

> **North-reading angles cover the area shown in red**

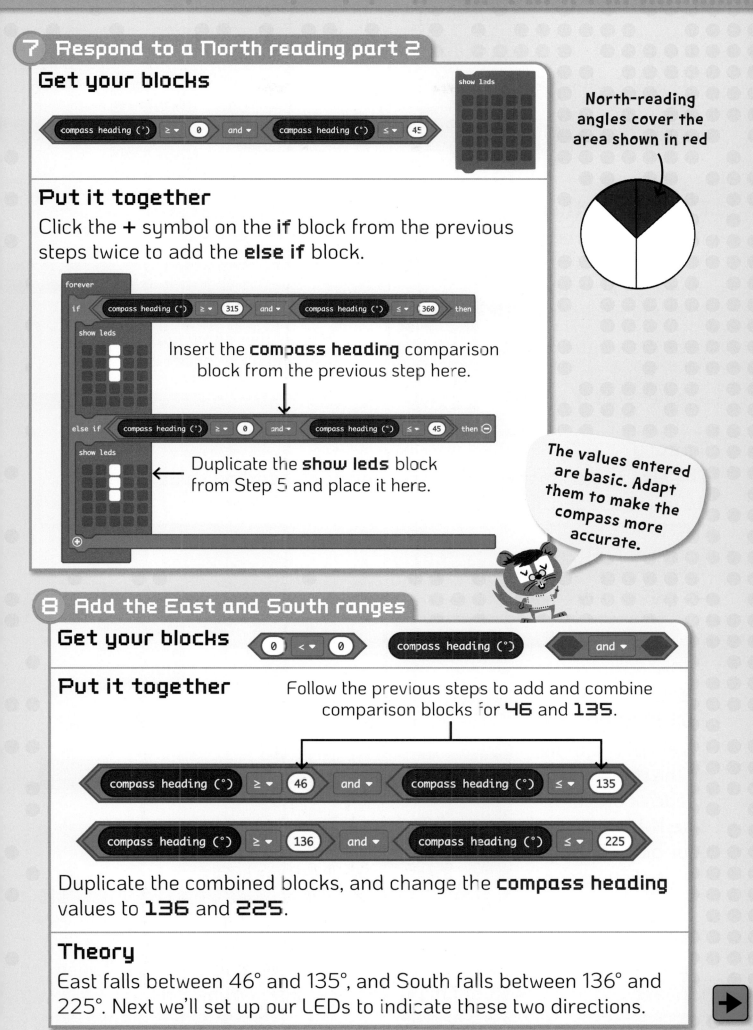

Put it together

Click the **+** symbol on the **if** block from the previous steps twice to add the **else if** block.

forever

if compass heading (°) ≥ ▾ 315 and ▾ compass heading (°) ≤ ▾ 360 then

show leds

Insert the **compass heading** comparison block from the previous step here.

else if compass heading (°) ≥ ▾ 0 and ▾ compass heading (°) ≤ ▾ 45 then ⊖

show leds

Duplicate the **show leds** block from Step 5 and place it here.

> The values entered are basic. Adapt them to make the compass more accurate.

8 Add the East and South ranges

Get your blocks

0 < ▾ 0   compass heading (°)   and ▾

Put it together

Follow the previous steps to add and combine comparison blocks for **46** and **135**.

compass heading (°) ≥ ▾ 46 and ▾ compass heading (°) ≤ ▾ 135

compass heading (°) ≥ ▾ 136 and ▾ compass heading (°) ≤ ▾ 225

Duplicate the combined blocks, and change the **compass heading** values to **136** and **225**.

Theory

East falls between 46° and 135°, and South falls between 136° and 225°. Next we'll set up our LEDs to indicate these two directions.

9 Respond to an East reading

Get your blocks

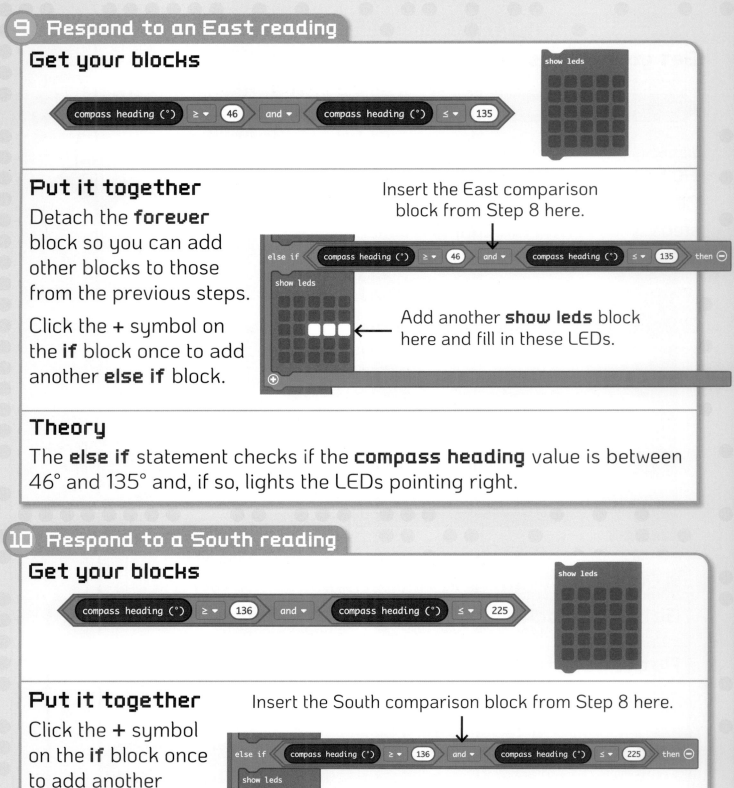

Put it together

Detach the **forever** block so you can add other blocks to those from the previous steps.

Click the + symbol on the **if** block once to add another **else if** block.

Insert the East comparison block from Step 8 here.

Add another **show leds** block here and fill in these LEDs.

Theory

The **else if** statement checks if the **compass heading** value is between 46° and 135° and, if so, lights the LEDs pointing right.

10 Respond to a South reading

Get your blocks

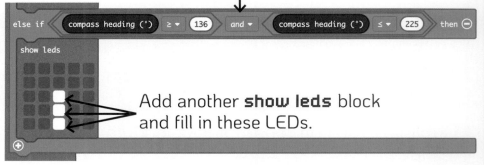

Put it together

Click the + symbol on the **if** block once to add another **else if** block to your blocks from the previous steps.

Insert the South comparison block from Step 8 here.

Add another **show leds** block and fill in these LEDs.

Theory

The **else if** statement checks if the **compass heading** value is between 136° and 225° and, if so, lights the LEDs pointing downwards.

11 Respond to a West reading

Get your blocks

show leds

Put it together

Add one more **show leds** block to the **else** block.

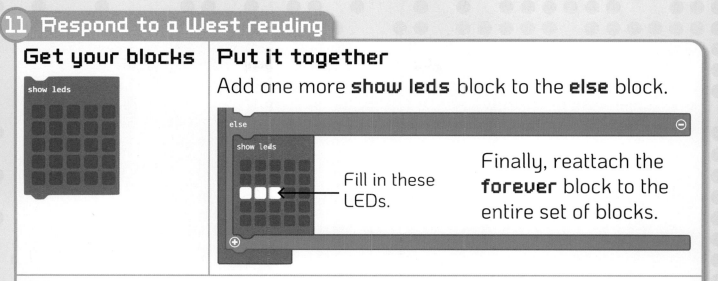

Fill in these LEDs.

Finally, reattach the **forever** block to the entire set of blocks.

Theory

Because West is the last direction, we use an **else** statement to respond to any **compass heading** values outside the ranges we've specified. If the micro:bit is facing westwards, it lights the LEDs pointing left.

12 Run the program

Put it together

Make sure to follow the calibration process from Step 1. Once calibrated, the micro:bit will work as a real-time compass.

Download the program code to your micro:bit.

on start

calibrate compass

Try this

Add angles for other compass directions, such as northeast or southwest.

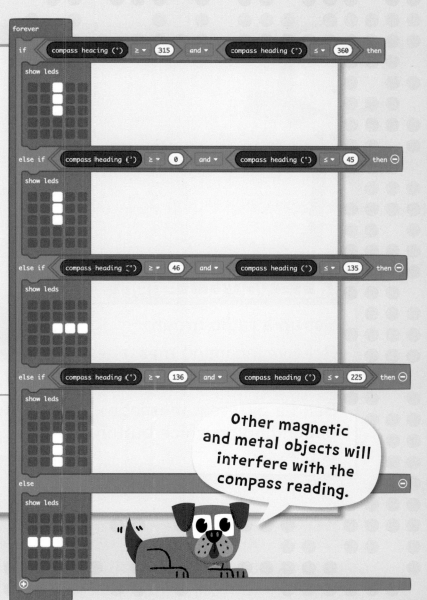

Other magnetic and metal objects will interfere with the compass reading.

Project 9 >
Radio communication

Using two micro:bits, send images and text from one micro:bit to the other using radio signals. You'll write two sets of code: one for the sender micro:bit and one for the receiver micro:bit.

From me...

To you...

SKILLS YOU'LL LEARN

- Set up a radio group
- Receive incoming messages
- Validate incoming messages
- Send a different message depending on which button is pressed

WHAT YOU'LL NEED

- Two micro:bits
- Two battery packs
- Four AAA batteries

Note: This project requires two micro:bits. If you only have access to one, you can use the multi-editor website (**https://makecode.com/multi-editor/**) to simulate having two, but you cannot radio from a simulator to a real micro:bit.

1 Set the sender radio group

Get your blocks

on start

radio set group 1

Put it together

Combine the **radio set group** block from the **Radio** group with the **on start** block. Leave the **radio set group** value at **1**.

on start
radio set group 1

Theory

This program, which we'll call *sender*, sets the radio group to 1. This tells the micro:bit to broadcast to other micro:bits with a radio group of 1. You can set the radio group to any value between 1 and 255, but the value must match for the sender and receiver micro:bits.

Your radio programs should always start with this code.

2 Send a message

Get your blocks

on button A ▼ pressed

radio send number 0

Put it together

Combine the **on button pressed** block from the **Input** group with the **radio send number** block from the **Radio** group.

on button A ▼ pressed
radio send number 0

Theory

When you press button A, the sender micro:bit uses its built-in radio chip to transmit the number **0** to other micro:bits.

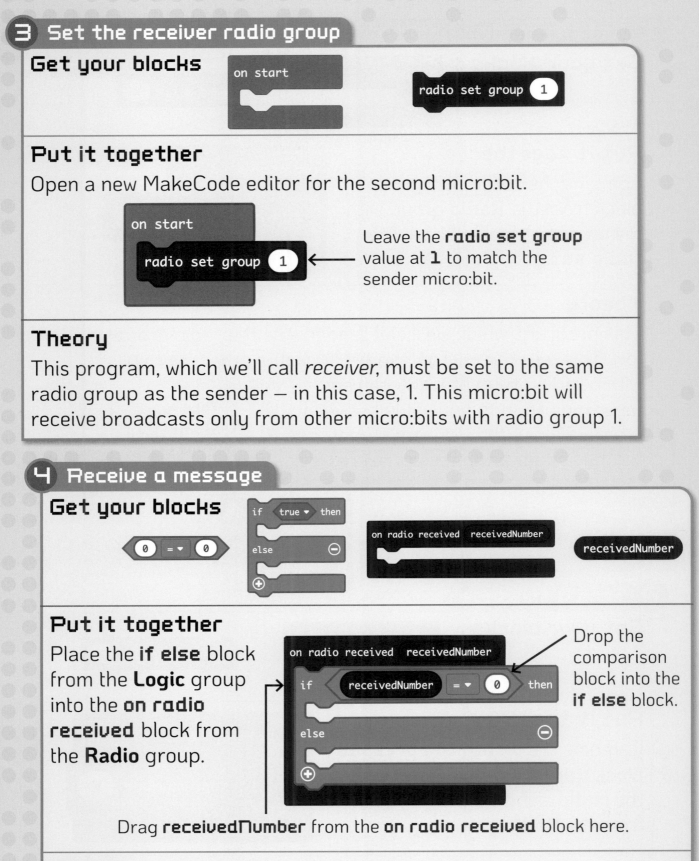

3 Set the receiver radio group

Get your blocks

on start

radio set group 1

Put it together

Open a new MakeCode editor for the second micro:bit.

on start
radio set group 1

Leave the **radio set group** value at **1** to match the sender micro:bit.

Theory

This program, which we'll call *receiver*, must be set to the same radio group as the sender — in this case, 1. This micro:bit will receive broadcasts only from other micro:bits with radio group 1.

4 Receive a message

Get your blocks

if true then
else

0 = 0

on radio received receivedNumber

receivedNumber

Put it together

Place the **if else** block from the **Logic** group into the **on radio received** block from the **Radio** group.

on radio received receivedNumber
if receivedNumber = 0 then
else

Drop the comparison block into the **if else** block.

Drag **receivedNumber** from the **on radio received** block here.

Theory

When the sender micro:bit transmits a number, the receiver micro:bit saves it in **receivedNumber**. The comparison block checks if the number is **0**, and if so, the **if else** statement triggers an event. We'll set that up next.

5 Display an image on the receiver

Get your blocks

show icon ▼   pause (ms) 100 ▼   clear screen

Put it together

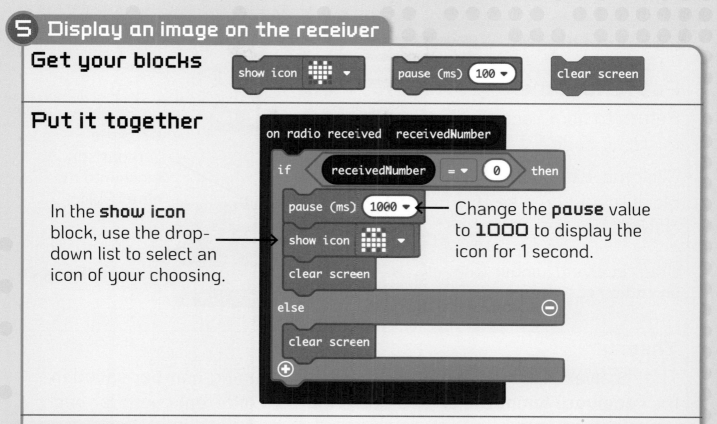

In the **show icon** block, use the drop-down list to select an icon of your choosing.

Change the **pause** value to **1000** to display the icon for 1 second.

```
on radio received  receivedNumber
    if  receivedNumber  = ▼  0  then
        pause (ms) 1000 ▼
        show icon ▼
        clear screen
    else
        clear screen
```

Theory

If the **receivedNumber** is **0**, the receiver micro:bit displays an icon on the LED grid for 1 second and then clears the screen. If the receiver micro:bit receives a number other than **0**, the **else** block will run. The **else** condition runs the code to clear the screen, so nothing is displayed.

6 Send a different message

Get your blocks

on button A ▼ pressed

radio send number 0

Put it together

Return to your sender micro:bit code.

Change the **on button pressed** value to **B**.

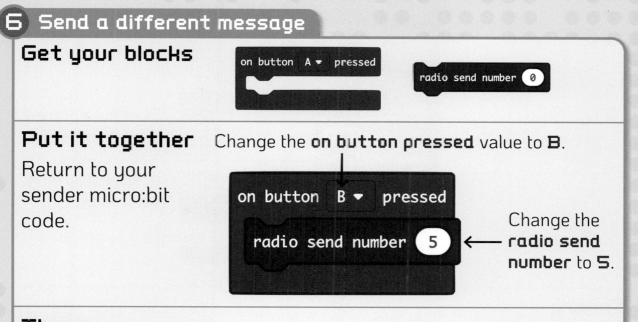

```
on button  B ▼  pressed
    radio send number  5
```

Change the **radio send number** to **5**.

Theory

When button B is pressed, the sender micro:bit transmits the number **5** to other micro:bits in the same radio group.

7 Check for the second message

Get your blocks

receivedNumber   ⟨ 0 ⟩ = ▾ ⟨ 0 ⟩

Put it together

Return to your receiver micro:bit code.

Click the **+** in the **if else** block to add an **else if** clause.

Drag **receivedNumber** from **on radio received** here.

Drop the comparison block into the **else if** block.

Change **receivedNumber** to **5**.

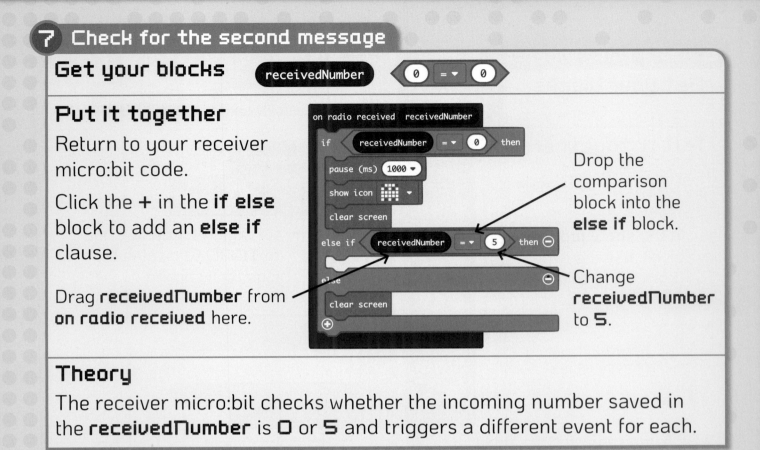

```
on radio received  receivedNumber
  if   receivedNumber  = ▾  0   then
    pause (ms) 1000 ▾
    show icon  ⊞  ▾
    clear screen
  else if   receivedNumber  = ▾  5   then ⊖
  else                                    ⊖
    clear screen
  ⊕
```

Theory

The receiver micro:bit checks whether the incoming number saved in the **receivedNumber** is **0** or **5** and triggers a different event for each.

8 Display a different image on the receiver

Get your blocks

show icon ⊞ ▾   pause (ms) 100 ▾   clear screen

Put it together

```
on radio received  receivedNumber
  if   receivedNumber  = ▾  0   then
    pause (ms) 1000 ▾
    show icon  ⊞  ▾
    clear screen
  else if   receivedNumber  = ▾  5   then ⊖
    pause (ms) 1000 ▾
    show icon  ▮  ▾
    clear screen
  else                                    ⊖
    clear screen
  ⊕
```

Choose a different icon to display for 1 second when the receiver micro:bit receives **5**.

Theory

The receiver micro:bit displays a different icon for 1 second depending on whether it receives **0** or **5**. If it receives neither, the screen remains clear.

9 Run the sender program

Download this program to the sender micro:bit. This code will enable you to control the receiver micro:bit.

```
on start
    radio set group    1
```

```
on button  A ▼  pressed
    radio send number    0
```

```
on button  B ▼  pressed
    radio send number    5
```

10 Run the receiver program

Download the program to the receiver micro:bit.

```
on start
    radio set group    1
```

```
on radio received    receivedNumber
    if    receivedNumber    = ▼    0    then
        pause (ms)  1000 ▼
        show icon  ▦ ▼
        clear screen
    else if    receivedNumber    = ▼    5    then ⊖
        pause (ms)  1000 ▼
        show icon  ▦ ▼
        clear screen
    else ⊖
        clear screen
    ⊕
```

Try this

- Send a third image when you press buttons A and B together.

- Use the **on shake** block to trigger an image to be displayed.

- Use the **radio send string** block to display text instead of images.

Project 10 >
Bag alarm

Using two micro:bits, set up an alarm system that detects when your bag is moved, and sends a warning from a sender micro:bit to a receiver micro:bit.

SKILLS YOU'LL LEARN

- Set a radio group
- Detect movement
- Broadcast a number
- Respond to an incoming message

WHAT YOU'LL NEED

- Two micro:bits
- Two battery packs
- Four AAA batteries
- Your school bag

1 Set the sender radio group

Get your blocks

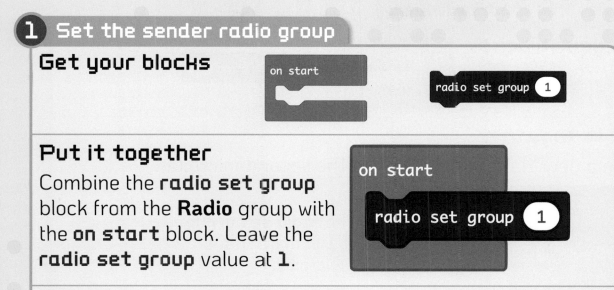

Put it together

Combine the **radio set group** block from the **Radio** group with the **on start** block. Leave the **radio set group** value at **1**.

Theory

This program, which we'll call *sender*, sets the radio group to 1. This tells the micro:bit to broadcast to other micro:bits with a radio group of 1. You can set the radio group to any value between 1 and 255, but the value must match for the sender and receiver micro:bits. Your radio programs should always start with this code.

2 Set a trigger signal

Get your blocks

Put it together

Combine the **on shake** block from the **Input** group with the **radio send number** block from the **Radio** group.

Select **logo up** from the drop-down list.

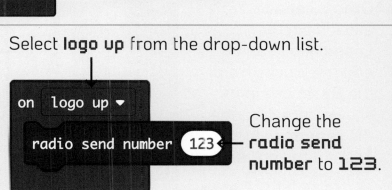

Change the **radio send number** to **123**.

Theory

The **logo up** block detects whether the bag is being lifted. If it is, the sender micro:bit sends the number **123** to the receiver micro:bit. This number triggers an alarm, alerting you that your bag has been moved. Next we'll look at the code for the receiver micro:bit.

3 Set the receiver radio group

Get your blocks

on start

radio set group 1

Put it together

Open a new MakeCode editor for the second micro:bit.

on start

radio set group 1

Leave the **radio set group** value at **1** to match the sender micro:bit.

Theory

This program, which we'll call *receiver*, must be set to the same radio group as the sender — in this case, 1. This micro:bit will receive broadcasts only from other micro:bits with radio group 1.

4 Set up a warning message

Get your blocks

show icon

pause (ms) 100 ▼

clear screen

repeat 10 times
do

Put it together

Drag a **repeat** block from the **Loops** group and add the blocks from the **Basic** group as shown here. Change the **repeat** value to **10** and the **pause** values to **1000**.

repeat 10 times
do
show icon
pause (ms) 1000 ▼
clear screen
pause (ms) 1000 ▼

In the **show icon** block, use the drop-down list to select the skull.

Theory

When the receiver micro:bit receives the warning message, the skull icon will display for 1 second and then clear. This alert repeats 10 times, making the skull flash.

5 Display the warning message

Get your blocks

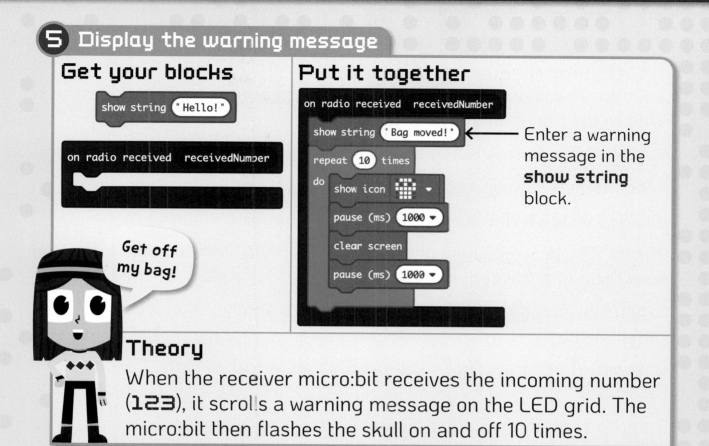

Put it together

Enter a warning message in the **show string** block.

Get off my bag!

Theory

When the receiver micro:bit receives the incoming number (**123**), it scrolls a warning message on the LED grid. The micro:bit then flashes the skull on and off 10 times.

6 Run the programs

Download the *sender* program to the sender micro:bit and the *receiver* program to the receiver micro:bit. Insert the batteries into the battery packs and connect one pack to each micro:bit. Place the sender micro:bit into your bag and set it aside. Keep the receiver micro:bit with you.

Sender program

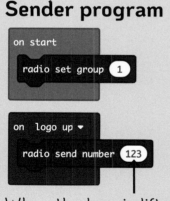

When the bag is lifted, it triggers the sender micro:bit to broadcast the number **123**.

Receiver program

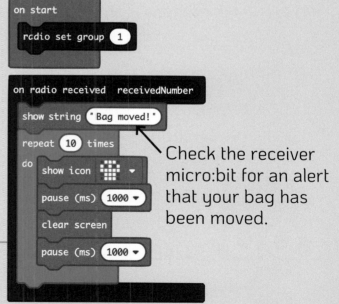

Check the receiver micro:bit for an alert that your bag has been moved.

Try this

- Experiment with different movements to see what works best for your set-up.

- Use **Music** blocks to add sound effects to your alarm.

Glossary

.hex file The .hex file contains data in a format that can be processed to write to the micro:bit's memory.

Acceleration Refers to the change in speed in the X, Y and Z directions.

Accelerometer A sensor that measures a change in speed or motion.

Analog A signal that has a continuously changing value.

Blocks These are chunks or blocks of pre-programmed code. Drag and drop them into the coding window to create a program for the micro:bit.

Broadcast Send data from one micro:bit to another via radio communication.

Browser A program that shows web pages — for example, Chrome or Safari.

Bug An error in the code that stops it from running correctly.

Calibrate Adjusting the measurements of the compass to ensure that readings are accurate.

Conditional A part of the program that tells the micro:bit to run certain actions when certain conditions are met.

Digital Information about a signal or data that is stored in a state, such as 0 or 1, On or Off.

Download Write the program code to the micro:bit.

Duplicate Make a copy of the code.

GND The ground pin used to complete a circuit, creating a continuous flow.

IF statement A block of code used to check if a certain condition is met.

Input Controlling the micro:bit — for example, by shaking it or pressing the buttons.

Interface A way for a human to interact with hardware such as computers and machines.

JavaScript A language that is used to create an interactive website.

LED Array A display of 25 red LEDs consisting of 5 individual rows of 5 LEDs.

LEDs Light-emitting diodes.

Loop A group of instructions that continually repeat.

Magnetometer A sensor for measuring the strength and direction of magnetic fields.

MakeCode editor A website that is used to code physical computing devices such as the micro:bit.

Micro USB cable A USB cable with a standard USB and a smaller connector.

micro:bit A pocket-sized computer that demonstrates how software and hardware work together.

Milliseconds 1/1000th of a second.

Output Feedback from the micro:bit as sound or displayed on the LEDs.

Pair/Pairing A method of connecting the micro:bit to a device so you can download program code.

Pins The micro:bit contains 25 gold-edge connectors referred to as pins. They provide input, output and power.

Program A set of instructions (blocks) that join together to make something happen.

Python An alternative programming language.

Radio group Similar to a channel on a TV. It ensures the micro:bit can only send or receive in one radio group at a time.

Random A number that cannot be guessed or predicted.

Simulator Allows you to run micro:bit programs in the web browser to test if they work correctly.

String Data in a program that can be letters, symbols, numbers, or even blank spaces.

USB Universal Serial Bus.

USB port Hardware that enables you to connect devices to a computer using a USB cable.

Variable A value that can change.

While A block of code that continues to repeat while a condition is met.

My notes >